JUDGES
& RUTH
A SELF-STUDY GUIDE

Irving L. Jensen

MOODY PRESS
CHICAGO

Cover photo: Hill of Moreh in northern Israel

ISBN: 0-8024-4484-9

3 5 7 9 10 8 6 4 2

Printed in the United States of America

Contents

Introduction   4

JUDGES
1. Background and Survey   6
2. Israel's Failure and Its Causes   18
3. First Judges   27
4. The Sword of the Lord and of Gideon   38
5. A Study in Contrasts: Abimelech and Jephthah   46
6. Birth of Samson   55
7. Exploits of Samson   60
8. Idolatry of Dan   67
9. Immorality and Lawlessness of Benjamin   72

RUTH
10. Story of Ruth   77
11. Teaching of Ruth   87
    Bibliography   91

Introduction

One purpose of this series of Bible study manuals is to encourage more of the do-it-yourself kind of study. The key part of each lesson is the section called ANALYSIS, where you the student are directed into various studies of your own. In this section charts and outlines appear frequently to help you see things as a whole and in relation to each other, and to offer a periodic "fix" on the passage being analyzed.

Among other methods and procedures of Bible study urged in the Analysis section are:

1. Paragraph-by-paragraph study. This should always precede verse-by-verse study, so that you will not get lost in the details of the Bible text.

2. Jotting things down. Someone has said that the pencil is one of the best eyes. Throughout the manual you are urged to record your observations. I have found the analytical chart to be a productive work sheet for organizing one's study of a chapter of the Bible. (The analytical chart method is described in detail in the book *Independent Bible Study*.)

3. Independent study. The emphasis here is always: first see for yourself what the Bible text says; then go to commentaries for help. COMMENTS, a section within each lesson, serves as such a commentary help. Do not read this section until you have finished your own study of the passage.

4. The Bible, your textbook. Whatever version of the Bible you use, you will find these things will enhance your study immeasurably:

(a) Making many notations on the pages of your Bible—underlining, cross references, notes, etc.

(b) Large print Bible text, with wide margins. Many such inexpensive Bibles are available.

5. Using different versions of the Bible. The King James Version is the one referred to throughout these study guides. Work mainly with one basic version, but refer to other versions for the valuable light they may shed on the meaning of a word or phrase that may seem unclear in the version you are using. Some recommended study versions are: *The New International Version, The New American Standard Bible,* and *The Everday Bible.*

The books of Judges and Ruth will be more meaningful if you have first studied the books preceding them in the Bible, for these books (especially Joshua) furnish a clear picture of the setting of Judges and Ruth.

Throughout your study of Judges and Ruth, continually ask this question, What does this teach me? When you learn a truth, hide it in your heart to obey it, and then join with the psalmist in saying, "Thy word have I hid in mine heart, that I might not sin against thee" (Ps. 119:11).

Lesson 1
Background and Survey

Its descriptions of human nature make Judges one of the saddest biblical books; some have called it the book of failure. Everything about the ending of the book of Joshua (which appears just before Judges in our canon) causes the reader to anticipate continued blessing upon God's people in the rest-land of their inheritance (read Joshua 24:19-28). But one does not proceed far into the account of Judges before he senses that all is not well. Although there are deliverances along the way, the tone of the book is predominantly one of oppression and defeat because "every man did that which was right in his own eyes" (21:25).

But there is more than that to the book. It includes the gospel of the grace of God, and it is our happy privilege to study this portion of God's Word to learn innumerable spiritual truths that God would teach us.

Before we make a survey study of Judges as a whole, let us first become acquainted with the background of the book.

I. BACKGROUND

A. Title

The title of the book is Judges, the Hebrew *Shophetim* (e.g., 2:16). These judges should not be confused with the ordinary judges of the theocracy who fulfilled judicial functions (Ex. 18:21-26). The main task of the *shophetim* was to deliver (3:9) God's people from the oppression of their enemies, usually by war, and then to rule the people during the era of peace.

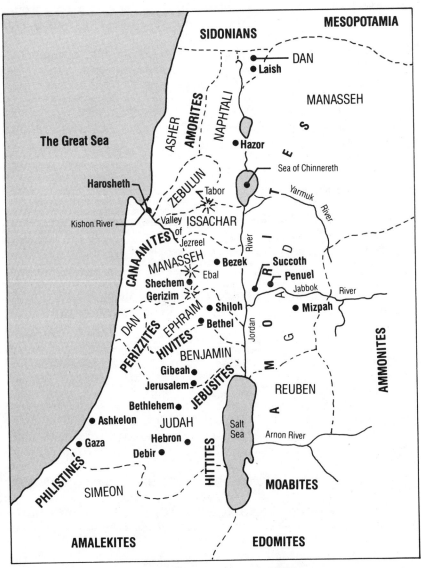

GEOGRAPHY OF THE BOOK OF JUDGES
(showing general locations of the enemy nations)

7

B. Date and Author

Judges was written and compiled by an unnamed prophet around 1000 B.C., not long after the death in 1051 B.C. of Samson, the last main character of the book. (Note: most of the dates used in this manual are those of John C. Whitcomb's chart "Old Testament Patriarchs and Judges.") The book was obviously written after Israel began to be ruled by a king, for the phrase "in those days there was no king in Israel" appears four times, implying that there was a king when the history was published (cf. 17:6; 18:1; 19:1; 21:25).

Jewish and early Christian tradition have assigned this book's authorship to Samuel. If the author was not Samuel, he was a contemporary of Samuel.

C. Israel's Enemies

From Joshua and Judges we learn that although Israel conquered the whole land of Canaan in a general sense there still remained pockets of enemy pagan nations here and there. These proved to be tests for the tribes of Israel as to whether they would obey God's command to subdue them utterly. Those were enemies within the boundaries of their inheritances. In addition to this, enemy nations from without also plagued the Israelites. The book of Judges shows how God used His appointed judges to conquer them. Refer to the map on page 7 for the locations of these enemy nations.

D. Place in the Bible

Judges, with its twenty-one chapters, takes up the narrative of Israel where the book of Joshua leaves it. The first verse makes this clear: "Now after the death of Joshua it came to pass . . ." (Judges 1:1).

In our Bible Judges is the seventh book, the second of the Historical Books. In the Hebrew Bible, Judges is seventh in the list, but it appears in the category called Former Prophets. It was classified as a prophetic book because, along with Joshua, Samuel, and Kings, it recorded the core of God's messages to His people in Canaan—blessing for obedience and cursing for disobedience —which was the essence of the preaching of the prophets who appeared a few hundred years later (e.g., Isaiah, Jeremiah).

This era of judges was one of many important phases of Israel's history, as shown in the chart on the following page.

Study the chart closely, for it represents all of Israel's history from Genesis to Malachi.

8

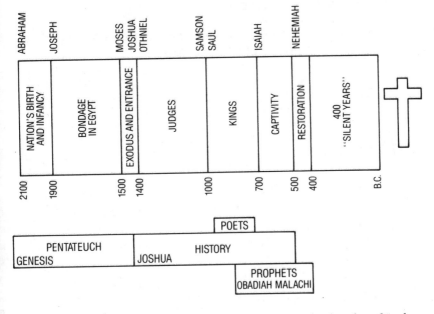

Many comparisons may be made between the books of Joshua and Judges, some of which are listed here:

JOSHUA	JUDGES
Upward trend, spiritually	Downward trend, spiritually
One man is prominent	No one man is prominent
Israel as a tutored child	Israel as an adult
Victory	Defeat
Fidelity	Apostasy

As the book of Joshua closes, Israel is shown taking a stand for God. Thus they entered into the promised blessings of the inheritance—victory, prosperity, and happiness—which is the life that God would ever have His people lead. They were still surrounded by enemies; indeed some enemies still lived within their boundaries. But if they would obey God's commands concerning these enemies, they would have the power of the Almighty with them.

In the book of Judges we see Israel turning away from God and doing the very things that God through Moses and Joshua had repeatedly besought them not to do.

E. Time Period of the Judges

The rule of the judges of this book (Othniel to Samson) extended for about three hundred twenty-five years. (Note: Eli, a priest-judge, and Samuel, a prophet-judge, do not appear in the Bible until 1 Samuel.) The following chart gives the order and dates of the reigns. Note how the three-chapter and four-chapter groups of the book of Judges cover these reigns.

DATES OF THE JUDGES

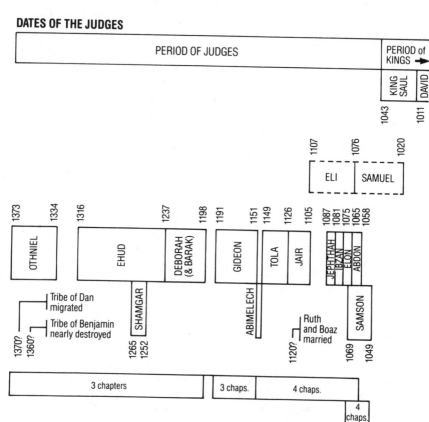

Begin now to become acquainted with the names of these judges, for they are the main characters of this Bible book.

II. SURVEY

Before we begin to analyze the individual parts of Judges, we should get a skyscraper view of the book as a whole. This is necessary procedure for getting the most out of Bible study.

A. Names of the Judges

Before making your first survey reading of the book, become more familiar with the names of the twelve judges. (Abimelech, false ruler, and Barak, appointee of Deborah, were not judges.) To do this, study the accompanying chart describing the judges. Consult the Scripture references for each judge. If possible, memorize the list of judges. Pronounce the names aloud, for a more lasting impression (use pronunciations given in a Bible dictionary, if necessary). Note the tribe from which each judge came. Try to associate the items with the correct names under *identification*. Refer to the map on page 7 for the locations of the enemy nations that the judges fought.

B. Structure of the Book

First swiftly scan the book, reading at least the first and last sentences of the chapters and also the chapter headings in your Bible. The purpose of this exercise is merely to catch highlights and to sense something of the tone of its message.

Next choose a chapter title for each chapter and record these on the chart on page 15. (Note the special segment divisions at 2:6; 3:7; and 12:8. Mark these divisions in your Bible before you get your chapter titles.)

Record also the names of all the judges cited in the book in the chapter spaces on the survey chart. In what group of chapters do these appear? To which judges is much of the space in the text devoted? Compare how much space in the text is used to tell of the periods of rest (e.g., 3:11) with the amount of space used to describe events in the ensuing oppressions.

What does this reveal of the purpose of the book of Judges?

_____

_____

After you have finished with the above phase of independent Bible study, proceed with the study guides that follow.

Judges is divided into three main parts. Study the accompanying chart closely. See how your own chapter titles fit into the outlines.

JUDGES OF ISRAEL

NAME	TRIBE	IDENTIFICATION	ENEMY	YEARS OF OPPRESSION	YEARS OF PEACE	REFERENCES	NOTES
1. OTHNIEL	Judah	nephew of Caleb	Mesopotamians (king Chushan)	8	40	3:9-11	
2. EHUD	Benjamin	left-handed an assassin	Moabites (king Eglon)	18	80	3:12-30	
3. SHAMGAR	Naphtali	used ox goad	Philistines	?	?	3:31	
4. DEBORAH	Ephraim	only woman judge	Canaanites (king Jabin)	20	40	4:4–5:31	
5. GIDEON	Manasseh	of an obscure family sought a sign	Midianites	7	40	6:11—8:35	
6. TOLA	Issachar				23	10:1-2	
7. JAIR	Gilead	30 sons, 30 cities			22	10:3-5	
8. JEPHTHAH	Gilead	made rash vow	Ammonites	18	6	11:1—12:7	
9. IBZAN	(Bethlehem)	30 sons, 30 daughters			7	12:8-10	
10. ELON	Zebulun				10	12:11-12	
11. ABDON	Ephraim				8	12:13-15	
12. SAMSON	Dan	Nazirite from birth strongest man	Philistines	40	20	13:2—16:31	

1. Read 1:1–3:6, and observe how these chapters serve as an introduction to the main body of the book. Why is a main division made at 3:7?

_____

_____

2. The one main clue suggesting that chapter 17 begins a new section in Judges (called here Double Appendix) is that chapter 16 records the last of the judges of the book, Samson. When we come to the study of chapters 17-21, we will make a survey study of that section.

3. The long section 3:7–16:31 is one continuous story of deliverances and setbacks, showing the principles of 1:1–3:6 in operation. Also, as shown by the chart, the section Double Appendix emphasizes the utter corruption of the years of the judges by citing further examples of sins committed during that period.

4. Note the contrast between the beginning of the book (fighting the enemy) and the end (fighting a brother). Watch for other comparisons and contrasts.

5. Two excellent key verses are 2:19 and 17:6 (or 24:25). In the course of your study be on the lookout for other key verses.

6. What important truths have you learned thus far from your study?

_____

_____

_____

_____

C. Theme

Two prominent lines of truth run through the entire book of Judges:

1. One is the desperate wickedness of the human heart, revealing its ingratitude, stubbornness, rebellion, and folly.

2. The other is God's long-suffering, patience, love, and mercy. No book in the Bible brings these two truths into sharper contrast—"the utter failure of Israel and the persistent grace of Jehovah."

1. *The Cycle of Israel's Religious Experience.* These two truths appear again and again in the book of Judges in a pattern that might be called a cycle, which is shown in the following diagram:

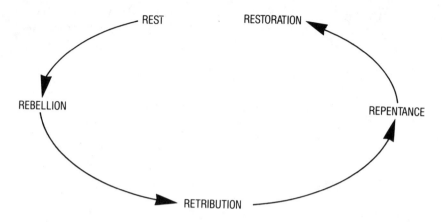

Read 2:16-19 to see the pattern of this cycle.

(a) REST. During Joshua's lifetime and for some years afterward, Israel served God and enjoyed the blessings of their restland. This is where the book of Judges begins.

(b) REBELLION. When a new generation arose, they divorced themselves from God and in rebellion against Him took on the ways of the Canaanites.

(c) RETRIBUTION. Just as He had said He would, God withdrew His protection and power from Israel and delivered them into the hands of their enemies.

(d) REPENTANCE. Then Israel repented of their sin and cried to God for help. (In 2:16 this is only implied; read 3:9 for a fuller statement. Read also 10:10 to see what was involved when they "cried unto the Lord.")

(e) RESTORATION. God raised up a judge to deliver His people from their oppressor and to lead them back to a life of fellowship with Him, back to the beginning of the cycle, REST.

At least seven times in the book of Judges this program is enacted. Seven times they forsook God, seven times He punished them, seven times they repented, and seven times He delivered them.

2. *The God of the Book of Judges.* The Old Testament is rich and full in its revelation of who God is. In your study of Judges you will learn much about God—*your* God. There is no one human hero in Judges. The real hero is the Lord. He is shown to be almighty in strength but tender in heart, persevering in grace but unyielding in wrath and judgment, diverse in His ways but simple and clear in His commands. He is the sovereign Director of the history of all peoples, the holy God condescending to sinful man and moving among them, supremely desiring to gain their hearts

JUDGES

Key verses:
2:19, 17:6

FIGHTING
THE ENEMY
"Who shall go up
for us against
the Canaanites?"
1:1

APOSTASIES OF GOD'S PEOPLE

300 YEARS of APOSTASIES, OPPRESSIONS, and DELIVERANCES

DEBORAH GIDEON SAMSON

INTRODUCTION	HISTORY of the JUDGES	DOUBLE APPENDIX
FAILURE CAUSES	APOSTASIES, OPPRESSIONS and DELIVERANCES	IDOLATRY of DAN / IMMORALITY and LAWLESSNESS of BENJAMIN
PRINCIPLES OPERATIVE	APOSTASIES, OPPRESSIONS, and DELIVERANCES	FURTHER EXAMPLES of CORRUPTION CITED

1:1 NEITHER DID ... DRIVE OUT 2:6

3:7 4:1 5 6 7 8 9 10 11:1 12:8 13:1 14 15 16 17 18 19 20 21

FIGHTING
A BROTHER
"Which of us
shall go up first . . .
against . . . Benjamin?"
20:18

15

and to be their Lord. As you study Judges open your heart to a deeper and more intimate knowledge of the Lord your God. (Note: the word *Lord* appears 178 times, and *God* appears 62 times in Judges.)

D. Spiritual Applications

The gospel (glad tidings) of Judges is that of restoration rather than regeneration. From the book of Joshua we learn how to appropriate the blessings of victorious Christian living (we in Christ and Christ in us); Judges spells out the woes of walking outside this fellowship with Christ and tells how to be restored.

Other valuable lessons are to be learned from Judges. Four of them are:

1. *God's people live far below their privileges.* The book of Joshua shows the high calling of Israel, the power and wealth and blessing that they enjoyed while being true to God. Judges shows the terrible unfaithfulness of Israel and their consequent weakness, failure, and poverty. Joshua shows how Israel might have lived. Judges shows how they actually did live.

The church is living below her privileges. The book of Acts shows how the church did live for a time under the direction of the Holy Spirit and how she might have continued to live if He had been allowed to rule, unhindered by sin and worldliness. But church history shows how she actually has lived.

2. *God gives the victory.* Victories are won "not by might, nor by power, but by my spirit, saith the Lord of hosts" (Zech. 4:6).

Throughout the history of the judges it will be observed that Israel had no might and no power in themselves. It was only when God raised up a man to lead—"and the Spirit of the Lord came upon him"—that Israel was delivered from the oppression of their enemies.

If the church is to win victories she must not depend upon her own wisdom, education, money, influence, or plans but upon the Holy Spirit.

3. *God uses weak things.* "Not many wise men after the flesh, not many mighty, not many noble, are called" (1 Cor. 1:26).

This statement of Paul's is richly illustrated in the choice of the judges. God selected the weak things to confound the mighty: a woman, an ox goad, a jawbone of an ass. Is was only by the Spirit of God that these weak instruments became mighty.

4. *God's people are to be lights.* God intended Israel to be a peculiar people, separate from all nations of the earth, uniquely His redeemed ones. Amid the abominations of idolatrous nations, this nation was to be a beacon—pure, holy, separate, pointing all

16

people to the one true God. God intends His church to occupy the same position in this age, and He would have every individual member of the church aspire to this position. Let each of us ask, "Am I occupying the place where it is God's will for me to be?"

III. REVIEW

We have considered many aspects of Judges in this lesson. Review the items studied thus far before you proceed to study the smaller individual parts of the book in the following lessons. Above all, be sure that you understand how the message of Judges applies basically to your own life so that you will be alert to catch its many applications along the way.

Lesson 2

Israel's Failure and Its Causes

This section of Judges furnishes the setting for the major part of the book that follows (see 3:7–16:31). First is recorded how the tribes of Israel failed to drive out all the enemy nations within their borders (1:1–2:5); then the causes are given (2:6–3:6). From this section we also learn the principles underlying the subsequent experiences of Israel's history during the times of the judges. (Note: this lesson may be studied in two separate units.)

I. ANALYSIS

A. Failure (1:1–2:5)

The organization of this segment is not too obvious. Study the accompanying analytical chart first; then read this passage carefully. As you proceed in your study, which will include following the suggestions given below, record observations on the chart. You are at liberty to choose what you will record, but be sure to record something. The value of jotting things down cannot be overemphasized.

1. Underline in your Bible references to the enemy nations such as the Canaanites. Locate names of cities on a good map. Do not overlook this step, for it will greatly help you to appreciate why God commanded the enemy inhabitants to be routed. Observe how many cities of the enemies were still scattered throughout Canaan.

2. See 1:1. How is this verse related to what happened before in Joshua and to what follows?

18

JUDGES 1:1—2:5

DETERMINATION	1:1
- - - - - - - - -	- - - - - - - - -
OBEDIENCE —enemy driven out—	1:2
	1:21
	22
	27
	29
DISOBEDIENCE —enemy remains—	30
	31
	33
	34
- - - - - - - - -	- - - - - - - - -
REMORSE	2:1
WEEPING	
	2:5

19

Contrast the phrase "asked the Lord" with the last verse of Judges.

---

3. See 1:2-20. Make a list of the various causes of the successes of the tribes of Judah and Simeon. (Note: references to tribes are often personified in the Old Testament, e.g., "And Judah said unto Simeon his brother," 1:3.)

What important truths do these verses teach?

Record key words and phrases on your analytical chart.
4. See 1:21-36. Compare "could not drive out" (1:19) with "did not drive out" (1:21).

What key phrase in repeated throughout this paragraph?

Does it appear from the text that the Israelites made any attempt to drive out the enemies? What may we conclude from this?

---

5. See 2:1-5. How is this paragraph an appropriate conclusion to the segment?

Bochim ("weepers") was a town probably situated between Bethel and Shiloh. Analyze this paragraph carefully. Record your observations on the analytical chart. What do the verses teach about God?

Observe the phrase "angel of the Lord." This phrase appears more often in Judges than in any other book of the Bible. (You may want to consult an exhaustive concordance to compare other appearances of the phrase.) As to who the angel of the Lord was, "there is good reason for thinking that He is the pre-incarnate Logos, his appearance in angelic or human form foreshadowing His coming in the flesh."[1] Keep this in mind as you come across the phrase in Judges.

B. Causes (2:6–3:6)

This segment complements the earlier one in furnishing the setting for Judges. In these verses we learn the causes for Israel's failure to appropriate the blessings of Canaan, God's rest-land.

First, mark these paragraph divisions in your Bible: 2:6, 11, 16; 3:1. Read carefully through the segment a few times, paragraph by paragraph. Underline key words and phrases. Look for related things. Observe the contrasts. Make a special note of things that strike you for the first time.

Now begin to record your observations on an analytical chart. Use the accompanying chart as a starting point. In your study you should first see the larger outline of the segment and then proceed to the smaller details.

1. How do the first and last paragraphs serve as introductory and concluding paragraphs, respectively?

_____

_____

2. See 2:6-10. Compare these verses with Joshua 24:28-31. Why are the verses repeated here?

_____

How does verse 10 introduce all that follows?

_____

Record on your chart what the new generation "knew not." What significant spiritual truths lie behind these words?

_____

_____

3. See 2:11-15. What is the connection between the words "forsook" and "followed" in verse 12?

_____

_____

1. Merrill C. Tenney, ed., *The Zondervan Pictorial Bible Dictionary* (Grand Rapids: Zondervan, 1963), p. 40.

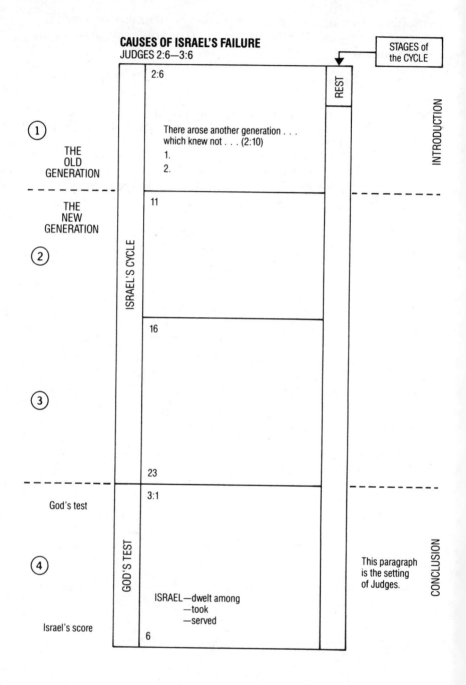

CAUSES OF ISRAEL'S FAILURE
JUDGES 2:6—3:6

STAGES of
the CYCLE

REST

INTRODUCTION

① THE OLD GENERATION

2:6

There arose another generation . . .
which knew not . . . (2:10)
1.
2.

THE NEW GENERATION

② ISRAEL'S CYCLE

11

③

16

23

④ GOD'S TEST

God's test

3:1

ISRAEL—dwelt among
—took
—served

Israel's score

6

This paragraph
is the setting
of Judges.

CONCLUSION

Notice how the idea is repeated in verse 13. Contrast "they forsook the Lord" (v. 13) with "neither delivered he them [nations]" (v. 23).

Which of the Ten Commandments were the Israelites breaking? Record key words and phrases on your chart.

The Baals were the presiding fertility gods of the various pagan communities and were worshiped as the gods responsible for productivity in human life and the animal kingdom as well as in the fruit of the land. The Ashtaroth were the fertility goddesses of these nations, consorts of the Baals. Why would the people have revered these gods so highly?

What strong temptations cause Christians to walk away from the fellowship of the Lord and to serve other gods?

---

4. See 2:16-23. This paragraph introduces us to the pattern of cycle in the Israelites' religious experience. Beginning with the word REST, record the stages of the cycle (Lesson 1) in the appropriate places in the right-hand vertical column. (The cycle begins with the first paragraph.) Note that there is no explicit reference to repentance. Where would repentance be in the cycle? (Cf. 3:9a with 2:15b.)

How is God's covenant related to His commandments? (2:20)

---

5. See 3:1-6. How is this paragraph related to the preceding one?

For the ambiguous King James reading of verse 2, substitute this translation (Berkeley): "so that the generations of the Israelites, who had experienced no wars, might become versed in the arts of war." Notice the key word "prove" in this paragraph. Why did God want to prove the Israelites?

How did they respond to the test?

What were the sins of 3:5-6?

Compare 3:6 with 2:6. What made the difference?

Record on your chart some of the causes of Israel's failure. (Record one per paragraph.) What does this passage teach about the nature of God? What does it teach about sinful human nature? Write a list for each.

II. COMMENTS

From the first two verses of chapter 1 it appears that the holy war was resumed as a result of the influence of Joshua's last address. An attempt was made to exterminate the condemned nations that should have been driven out long before. By God's direction, Judah and Simeon took the lead, with the other tribes following their example, and went up and fought the enemy in his territory.

But then the record of Judges takes a turn and begins to tally the failures of the tribes: "Judah; . . . could not drive out the inhabitants of the valley" (1:19); "the children of Benjamin did not drive out the Jebusites" (1:21); "neither did Manasseh drive out the inhabitants of Beth-shean" (1:27); "neither did Ephraim drive out the Canaanites" (1:29); "neither did Zebulun drive out the inhabitants of Kitron" (1:39); "neither did Asher drive out the inhabitants of Accho" (1:31); "neither did Naphtali drive out the inhabitants of Beth-shemesh" (1:33); "and the Amorites forced the children of Dan into the mountains" (1:34).

Why such failure? Judges 2:1-3 gives the reason. It was not God's fault but Israel's, as He plainly pointed out to them.

Actually, the enemy nations remaining within the boundaries of the tribes of Israel served the purposes of God in various ways:

1. Originally, God allowed some of these nations to escape the conquest program of Joshua in order that the land in those parts would not suddenly be left unattended and thus become desolate. Israel was to drive out the enemies only "little by little" (Deut. 7:20-24).

2. The presence of the enemies was a daily test for the Israelites as to whether they would obey the command of the Lord to drive them out and have nothing to do with them and their gods, or whether they would choose the way of least resistance, "let well enough alone," and yield to the temptation of intermarrying with the nations and partaking of their licentious religious rites (2:21-23; 3:4).

3. Every time the Israelites disobeyed God's command regarding their enemies, God used these enemies to punish and plunder His people, to their utter pain and distress (2:14-15).

4. One beneficial by-product resulted from the battles between the Israelites and their enemies. It was for the benefit of the Israelites that their new generation that had no experience in warfare was learning its art for any future defense needs (3:2).

The setting for the first of the judges (Lesson 3) is the sin and rebellion described in 3:5-6, with Israel dwelling among its enemies, intermarrying with them, and beginning to worship their gods.

What a sad position for this nation, which, so short a time before, took its stand with Joshua and repeatedly affirmed, "We will serve the Lord." It reminds us of the terrible lapse into idolatry at Mount Sinai, where, some time previously, the people had vowed to Moses: "All that the Lord hath said will we do, and be obedient" (Ex. 24:7).

Instead of recognizing the presence of these enemies among them as an opportunity to war against them and to prove their willingness to obey God's command to drive them out, Israel "dwelt among them" contentedly, "took their daughters to be their wives and gave their daughters to their sons." Worst of all, they "served their gods," forgetting the Lord their God and serving Baalim and the groves. It is no wonder that the anger of the Lord was hot against them.

25

III. SUMMARY

In 2:2-3 the chapters studied in this lesson about Israel's failure and its causes are summarized. These two verses might be reconstructed thus:

Israel failed to rid themselves
    (a) of the thorns in their sides (evil nations) and
    (b) of the snares of their paths (pagan gods),
because Israel did not obey the voice of the Lord
    (a) to avoid leagues with the nations and
    (b) to throw down their altars.

Let every Christian weep, as did the Israelites at Bochim, over disobedience to God.

Judges 3:7–5:31

First Judges

U p to this point in the book of Judges the record has been one of
a general introductory nature. Now we come to the beginning
of the main section of Judges that reports specific episodes of
apostasies, oppressions, and deliverances during three centuries
of reigns of judges over Israel. (Review the survey chart of Lesson
1 in order to fix in your mind the setting of the chapters of the
present lesson.)

I. ANALYSIS

First acquaint yourself with the geographical locations of the following important places named in these chapters (use the map on
page 7 and also consult the atlas that you are using for these studies): Mesopotamia, Moab, Philistia, regions of the Canaanites and
Ammonites, Hazor, Mount Tabor, Kishon river, Harosheth, Kedesh, Bethel, mountains of Ephraim, and boundaries of the twelve
tribes.

Now read 3:7–5:31 in one sitting. Keep pencil or pen in hand
as you read, marking such things as: references to sin, oppression,
repentance, deliverance, judges, and rest; key words and phrases;
references to the Lord. Look for the recurrence of the "cycle" dis-
cussed in Lesson 1.

Note in the accompanying illustration that the four oppressions came in a clockwise sequence from the surrounding places.
Thus, the first three were from outside the boundaries of Israel's
tribes and the fourth from within. What does this illustrate regarding God's ways in punishing and testing?

Review the chart *Dates of the Judges* (Lesson 1). Recall that
Shamgar was a contemporary of Ehud (see 5:6-7). (Some hold
that Shamgar and Deborah judged during the same period. Cf.
3:31.)

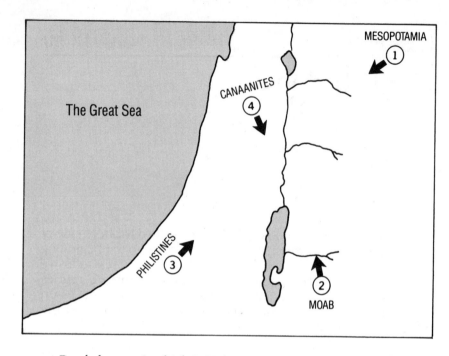

Read chapter 5, which is Hebrew poetry, as a song, noting the variety of pictures used to relate the historical account of chapter 4. Then make a list of your impressions and observations of prominent items.

We must not lose sight of the main purpose for studying Old Testament history. The apostle Paul wrote, "Now all these things happened unto them for examples: and *they are written for our admonition*, upon whom the ends of the world are come" (1 Cor. 10:11, emphasis added). But Old Testament narratives with their numerous facts of persons, places, and events are often only *partly* studied at the most because the organization or structure of the narrative is not always clear to the Bible student. The guides to analysis given in these study manuals—using such visual aids as analytical and survey charts—are intended to help you see more clearly the *total* story, without getting lost in the details. This should encourage you to press for the maximum spiritual admonitions.

Study the accompanying chart of this passage of Scripture. Observe that the song of Deborah and Barak (chap. 5) follows closely the outline of the historical account of the oppression under the Canaanites (chap. 4). On the chart each paragraph of the

THE FIRST FOUR OPPRESSIONS of ISRAEL
JUDGES 3:7—5:31

OPPRESSORS	① MESOPOTAMIANS	② MOABITES	③ PHILISTINES	④ CANAANITES				
					OPPRESSION	MOBILIZATION	BATTLE	SISERA	CONCLUSION
SIN	3:7	3:12	3:31	4:1	4:4	4:11	4:17	4:23-24
OPPRESSION								
CRY						"YOU GO . . . / I WILL"		
DELIVERANCE								
REST								
JUDGES	OTHNIEL	EHUD	SHAMGAR	DEBORAH				

PRAISE and SETTING	MOBILIZATION	BATTLE	SISERA	CONCLUSION
5:1	5:12	5:19	5:24	5:31

SONG of DEBORAH and BARAK

29

song (poetry) is placed under the parallel paragraph of the history (prose). In your study, read the parallel paragraphs together.

Return now to the beginning of the passage of this lesson (3:7), and analyze the paragraphs more closely. Use the following suggestions, recording key items on your chart.

1. For each of the oppressions, observe the references to:

the sin	(rebellion)
the oppression	(retribution)
the cry	(repentance)
the deliverance	(restoration)
the rest	(rest)
the death of the judge	

2. Note any statements that account for the successes of the judges. Why did the people revert to their evil ways when a judge died?

_____

_____

What does this teach?

_____

3. Ehud said to Eglon, "I have a message from God unto thee" (3:20). Was Ehud lying? If not, what was he really saying?

_____

_____

Were the slayings of Eglon (3:21) and Sisera (4:21) justified?

_____

_____

4. Shamgar's slaying of the six hundred Philistines was a miraculous feat. What other miracles are cited in these chapters?

_____

_____

_____

Concerning Shamgar's ox goad, "The ox goad might have been as long as eight feet. At one end it had a spike, and on the other a chisel-shaped blade, which was used in cleaning the plow. When necessary, the ox goad could serve as a substitute for a spear."[1]

1. Charles F. Pfeiffer and Everett F. Harrison, eds., *The Wycliffe Bible Commentary* (Chicago: Moody, 1962), p. 241.

5. *Chapter 4.* Notice especially references to God in the paragraphs of this chapter. Study this couplet of 4:6-7:
"[You] go and draw toward mount Tabor, . . ."
"I will draw unto thee . . ."
Throughout the dark pages of Judges you will find the references to God are the bright shining lights. List some important spiritual lessons taught in this chapter.

---

6. *Chapter 5.* When you are acquainted with the action of chapter 4, this chapter is fascinating reading because it contains the reflections of Deborah and Barak on the battle just won. If possible, read this chapter in other versions (e.g., Berkeley, *New American Standard Version*) for help in some of the ambiguous lines of the poem. Read the parallel paragraph of chapter 4 before studying the associated paragraph of chapter 5.
7. See 5:1-11. Observe the different words of praise. Apply 5:2*b* to Christian living.

---

8. See 5:12-18. Notice the lists of tribes that helped in the battle (5:14-15*a*; 18) and tribes that did not help (5:15*b*-17). (Note: Machir refers to the half tribe of Manasseh west of the Jordan.) What spiritual lessons can be learned from this paragraph?

---

9. See 5:19-27. Observe how verses 20 and 21 describe the storm that was the key to Israel's victory. Do Deborah and Barak claim the glory of victory? Contrast the curse of 5:23 with the blessing of 5:24.

---

10. See 5:28-31. What is the intent of this last stanza of Deborah's song?

Reflect on the pathos of a waiting mother, ignorant of judgment. Compare this with similar instances in Scripture, for example Matthew 25:41-46.

11. Write a list of five important truths these chapters of Judges teach.

II. COMMENTS

Prominent points concerning the first four judges are compiled in the following comments.

A. Othniel

As punishment for Israel's idolatry described in 3:5-6, God allowed the king of Mesopotamia, Chushan-rishathaim ("doubly wicked Chusham"), to oppress Israel. For eight years Israel served this foreigner. It was not as pleasant to serve him as to serve the Lord, so they soon cried to the Lord to deliver them.

Othniel, Caleb's nephew, was the first of the judges whom God raised up to deliver Israel. Othniel, by bravery in war, had won Caleb's daughter for his wife (Joshua 15:16-17), but it was not Othniel's strength or bravery that now enabled him to deliver Israel. "The Spirit of the Lord came upon him, . . . and the Lord delivered Chusham-rishathaim king of Mesopotamia into his hand" (3:10). So it was the Lord, as always, who delivered the children of Israel out of their difficulties.

Caleb was from the tribe of Judah. So we see that this tribe, which was first in the march (Num. 10:11-14), first in war (Judges 1:1-2), and alas, first in sin (Achan, Joshua 7:16-18), was the first to bring forth a deliverer.

B. Ehud

After the deliverance under Othniel, the land had rest from war forty years—one generation. But in 3:12 we read this sad refrain that seven times darkens the pages of the book of Judges: "And the children of Israel did evil again in the sight of the Lord." (Cf. 2:11; 3:7; 4:1; 6:1; 10:6; 13:1)

This time God used Moab, a nation to the southeast of Canaan, as His rod to chastise Israel for this second apostasy. Forming an alliance with the Ammonites and the Amalekites, the king of Moab swept over the territory occupied by Reuben and Gad, on the east of Jordan, advanced across the river, and made Jericho, "city of palm trees," their garrison. The position of Jericho enabled Moab to cut off the northern tribes of Israel from the southern tribes, and for eighteen years they reduced Israel to servitude, compelling them to pay tribute (3:12-14). At last Israel remembered that their God had helped them out of difficulties before. When they cried unto the Lord, He mercifully raised up another deliverer, Ehud.

Ehud, a left-handed man from the small tribe of Benjamin, was the second judge of Israel (3:15). God used him to deliver His people as well as He used the strong, brave Othniel of the leading tribe, Judah. The instrument as such was of no importance. What was important and necessary was that God worked in and through the instrument. He wanted to teach Israel that deliverance was wholly of faith.

The rebellion and victory of Israel took the Moabites completely by surprise and found them thoroughly unprepared. Ehud had brought a present, or the usual tribute, to King Eglon at Jericho. After dismissing the men who carried it, he professed to have a secret errand to the king—a message from God. Little did Eglon think it was the message of death. As he arose from his seat to receive God's message, Ehud's dagger was plunged to the hilt into his vitals; he was left alone to die, locked in his summer parlor. The delay in finding the body of the dead king afforded Ehud an escape to Seirath (located in the "mountain of Ephraim," which was the central mountain range of Palestine). There he blew a trumpet, summoning Israel to war. Before long Israel's army had taken the fords of Jordan, preventing the escape of the soldiers who held Jericho and also blocking Moabite reinforcements from the east. Ten thousand Moabites were slain that day.

This time the land had rest for eighty years.

C. Shamgar

We are told very little about the third oppression, this one by the hand of the Philistines, but no doubt God allowed it to come because of sin by Israel. The judge to deliver Israel this time was Shamgar, of whom we know only that he was the son of Anath and that with an ox goad he killed 600 Philistines (3:31).

The Philistines undoubtedly recognized the might of Shamgar as the power of the God of Israel and became panic-stricken. When one man, with only an ox goad for a weapon, was enabled to slay 600 men, what could not an army of men thus empowered do? They were wise to yield to God without further fighting. Shamgar "also delivered Israel" (3:31).

D. Deborah

One would naturally suppose that the experiences of one generation would be quite sufficient to teach the next generation the wisdom of serving God and the folly of going after idols. But so stubborn and perverse is the human heart that it is slow to learn from the experience of others. Each generation has to learn the lesson firsthand. And so at the beginning of chapter 4 we read, "And the children of Israel again did evil in the sight of the Lord."

After each deliverance the responsibility of the nation was increased, and the punishments grew more and more severe. This time the enemies were the Canaanites. For twenty years they mightily oppressed the people of Israel, who finally cried unto the Lord for help.

The Israelites refused to turn to the Lord until the bondage of their enemies became bitter and unbearable. When they were blessed and prosperous, they dallied with their enemies and trifled with the things that God had forbidden, only to wake up to find themselves absolutely in the power of these enemies. It was not until then that they felt their need of God's help.

Do we not see the counterpart of this line of action in some of God's children today? They will dally and trifle with habits, appetites, and temptations that are as dangerous to their progress and peace as were these enemies of Israel. They have seen the bondage and trouble of thousands who have made the same mistake in the past, yet they refuse to be warned and therefore must reap the consequences. When brought to the end of themselves they discover that this habit, appetite, or temptation has such a hold upon them that only God Himself can break its power.

And God is so merciful and patient. Even though His people repeatedly disobey Him, whenever they repent and cry unto Him, He always comes to the rescue. "If we confess our sins, he is faithful and just to forgive us our sins, and to cleanse us from all unrighteousness" (1 John 1:9).

God used a woman, Deborah, to deliver Israel from the Canaanite oppression. Deborah was fourth judge of Israel and the only woman to occupy the office. Again we are reminded that it is not by man's might, nor by his power, but by the Lord's Spirit (Zech. 4:6).

Jabin, king of Canaan, whose capital was the northern city of Hazor, had invaded and occupied the possessions of Naphtali, Zebulun, and Issachar. While Jabin ruled at Hazor, his general, Sisera, was stationed at the chief military post, Harosheth, with a large army so that he might hold the southern boundary of Jabin's newly acquired possessions.

For twenty years the Canaanites had oppressed Israel. Deborah the prophetess, living with her husband near Bethel, was judging Israel at that time. She received assurance of deliverance for the nation from the Lord. Summoning Barak, she disclosed the plan of action that God had given. Barak was to go to Mount Tabor, not many miles from Harosheth, with an army of ten thousand men. God would then cause Sisera to assemble all his forces at the Kishon river. Barak was to come down upon them from Mount Tabor, and God would deliver the Canaanites into his hand.

Either Barak had no confidence in the plan or felt that Deborah's presence was necessary to ensure success, for he insisted that she accompany him. Deborah consented but said that Barak would not have the honor of the undertaking, as Sisera would be slain by a woman. (This reveals something of Deborah's prophetic insight.)

The plan was carried out. Arriving at Kedesh, Barak called for the warriors of Zebulun and Naphtali; then he and Deborah proceeded with their army to Mount Tabor. Hearing of the movement, Sisera resolved to put a stop to any such attempt at rebellion. Barak had only ten thousand men. Sisera brought his mechanized army of nine hundred chariots of iron and his entire fighting force from Harosheth to the Kishon river. They formed a most formidable host in battle array in the valley there. Deborah on the mountain said to Barak, "Up; for this is the day in which the Lord hath delivered Sisera into thine hand: is not the Lord gone out before thee?" (4:14).

To get the full effect of the account of this battle, the song of Deborah and Barak (chap. 5) must be read. The record of 4:15—"And the Lord discomfited Sisera, and all his chariots, and all his host"—together with some expressions in the song make us conclude that as Barak came down upon the hosts of the Canaanites, a terrific storm burst upon them, throwing Sisera's army into confusion. "They fought from heaven; the stars in their courses fought against Sisera" (5:20).

The horses became unmanageable. In the trampling and plunging, the iron chariots upon which Sisera had been depending became instruments of destruction to his own men. The river, swollen by the torrents of water, swept away hundreds of the dead and dying. Sisera, to escape capture, alighted from his chariot and fled. Barak pursued Sisera's army, overtaking them at Harosheth, "and all the host of Sisera fell upon the edge of the sword; and there was not a man left" (4:16).

In the meantime, Sisera fled toward the capital. If only he could reach that city, he would be safe. But his strength was nearly gone, and, reaching the tent of the Kenite named Heber, he accepted the invitation of Heber's wife, Jael, to rest awhile.

Heber was descended from Hobab, whom Moses had invited to come into Canaan with the Israelites. Although Jael appeared friendly to Sisera, she was in reality loyal to Israel. Sisera was Israel's enemy and therefore her enemy. Since Jael was a woman, she could not meet Sisera in open fighting, but when he was asleep she killed him. When Barak came along on the trail of Sisera, Jael called him in and showed him the body.

One can hardly understand how a woman could emotionally bring herself to commit such a horrible act, a violation of hospitality and treachery to friendship. However, Jael's loyalty to God's people and the fulfillment of Deborah's prophecy that Sisera would be slain by a woman must not be overlooked. "The perfidy of Jael in ignoring rules of hospitality becomes less heinous if seen in the light of war's long record of brutality. . . . Jael's deed was considered an act of Israel, hence the manner in which Deborah gloated over it"[2] To understand all of the God-directed wars of His people in the Old Testament, one must see God as the sovereign Mover in history. Charles F. Pfeiffer writes, "Scripture does not abstract God from historical processes. The act of Jael is described, but the victory is ascribed to God. . . . God allows the heathen to chasten his people, and God raises up deliverers to save them. . . . It is not necessary to justify Jael's act. Even wicked deeds are represented in Scripture as furthering God's ultimate purposes (cf. Acts 2:23-24; Ps. 76:10)."[3]

This victory over the Canaanites was a great one. So utterly was their power broken that as a race they never attempted to regain their independence. After this, Israel seems to have pushed on northward, conquering the whole country occupied by the Canaanites.

2. Merrill C. Tenney, ed., *The Zondervan Pictorial Bible Dictionary* (Grand Rapids: Zondervan Publishing House, 1963), p. 400.
3. Pfeiffer and Harrison, p. 243.

III. SUMMARY

These chapters clearly reveal God's dealings with (1) His chosen people and (2) the enemies of His people.

The enemies of Israel were really enemies of God, for they made and worshiped other gods and would not turn to Him. For this Deborah could say, "So let all thine enemies perish, O Lord" (5:31).

God's chosen people were partakers of His covenant. Although they reaped oppression for turning away from Him, they were restored when they cried to Him in repentance. For this Deborah could sing, "Let them that love Him be as the sun when he goeth forth in his might" (5:31).

Lesson 4

The Sword of the Lord and of Gideon

These chapters about Gideon are three of the brightest and most interesting in the book of Judges. There seems to be no limit to the number of truths taught here. From these chapters comes the famous battle cry "The sword of the Lord and of Gideon!" Study this section carefully and prayerfully.

I. ANALYSIS

For the first stages of your analysis, follow the procedures of study suggested in earlier lessons. As you read the narrative, locate places on a map so that you can better visualize the action. Such places include Gaza, Ophrah (near Bethel), valley of Jezreel, hill of Moreh, Mount Gilead, Succoth, and Penuel. Keep in mind that the Midianites were nomads whose home base was the region east and southeast of the Dead Sea. At this time they were plaguing the Israelites in the south as far as the coastline by Gaza and in the north regions around the valley of Jezreel.

After the first reading, make an outline of the large groups in the story. Compare your outline with the following:

A. Midianite oppression and its cause	6:1-10
B. Gideon commissioned	6:11-32
C. Enemy's challenge and Gideon's response	6:33-35
D. Israel's mobilization	6:36–7:18
E. The battle	7:19–8:21
F. Aftermath	8:22-35

You will find it profitable to analyze especially these three segments, using the analytical chart:

6:1-10—paragraphs at verses 1, 3, 7
6:11-32—paragraphs at verses 11, 19, 25, 28
8:22-35—paragraphs at verses 22, 24, 29, 33

The following questions will suggest various approaches of study.

1. See 6:1-10. Compare this kind of oppression with the former ones. What was the main thrust of the prophet's message of 6:8-10?

_____

_____

2. See 6:11-24. Note the various promises given Gideon. Account for Gideon's questions of 6:13.

_____

Observe how God again chose a weak instrument to be His deliverer. What was Gideon thinking of when he made the exclamation of 6:22? (Read Ex. 33:20.)

_____

Jehovah-shalom means "The Lord is peace." Why was this an appropriate name for the altar?

_____

3. See 6:25-32. Gideon had raised an altar to the true God; now he is commanded to cast down an altar to the false gods. What spiritual truth is taught here?

_____

Gideon (literally "feller" or "hewer") was given another name, Jerubbaal, which means "Let Baal strive," as a result of this experience. How would this serve as a reminder to Gideon and Israel in future engagements with the enemy?

_____

4. See 6:33–7:18. Verse 34a may be translated "But the Spirit of the Lord *clothed* Gideon." In what way may it be said that the Spirit clothes Christians with power today? (Cf. Acts 1:8)

_____

_____

Gideon had already received a miraculous sign from God. Why did he seek more signs now?

_____

Why did God choose to let Gideon have only 300 warriors?

_____

What is symbolized by each of the items carried by the men: trumpets, pitchers, and lamps?

_____

What is the significance of the words "The sword of the Lord, and of Gideon"?

_____

_____

5. See 7:19–8:21. Observe the different instances of opposition to Gideon in this segment. How does internal dissension among God's people harm His work today?

_____

_____

6. See 8:22-35. Compare the Israelites' request of 8:22 with Gideon's answer of 8:23.

_____

_____

Note Gideon's blunder of 8:27. (The text does not say that Gideon sinned, though his action was the occasion for the sinful idolatry of the Israelites.) How is this a warning to all Christians, including Christian workers and leaders?

_____

_____

Baal-berith (8:33) means literally "Lord of the covenant." How was this an extreme case of idolatry for the Israelites?

_____

What important lessons may be learned from this last segment of chapter 8?

_____

_____

_____

II. COMMENTS

In chapter 6 Israel once more begins the same round of experience—sin, punishment, repentance, deliverance. In the first verse we read, "And the children of Israel did evil in the sight of the Lord." For this sin God allowed the Midianites to plague them.

This Midianite oppression was different from all the rest. Instead of occupying the land, the Midianites seem to have swarmed across the Jordan at unexpected times, bringing with them their cattle, tents, and camels. What they could not take away as spoil, they would destroy, leaving the country impoverished and the Israelites hiding in dens and caves for fear.

What a sad sight to see Israel burrowing like frightened rats in holes in their God-given land when they might have stood and faced the combined nations of the world and, in the name and power of their God, have compelled them to fall back. But Israel had sinned. That was the secret of their weakness and cowardice.

"And the children of Israel cried unto the Lord" (6:6). It was the only thing to do. But before God sent help this time, He sent a prophet to remind Israel of His past goodness and their own unfaithfulness. This prophet probably went up and down the land preaching to the people to repent. The outline or substance of his message is given in 6:8-10. No doubt Israel's readiness to respond to the summons of Gideon was due in some measure to the preaching of this prophet. Many in Israel must have been convinced of God's willingness and power to relieve their distress.

Gideon, the fifth judge of Israel, is a most interesting and instructive Bible character. A member of the tribe of Manasseh, he lived in the obscure village of Ophrah. Although all his relatives had become Baal worshipers, he remained obedient to God. When first we see him, Gideon is by the winepress threshing wheat that he might hide it before the next invasion of the dreaded enemies. Doubtless as he worked he thought with sadness of the condition of his country, perhaps meditating on some words he had heard the prophet say and sorrowing that the power of God was not with Israel then as in former times.

As he was thinking on these things, the angel of the Lord came and sat near him under an oak. He said to Gideon, "The Lord is with thee, thou mighty man of valour" (6:12). The context shows this to be another manifestation of the second Person of Trinity. (The phrase "an angel of the Lord" in 6:11, 22 is rightly translated "the angel of the Lord.") Gideon did not recognize Him to be the Lord Himself, nor did he observe the personal character of the message. He said, "Oh my Lord, if the Lord be with *us* [not 'me'] why then is all this befallen *us*? ... the Lord hath forsaken *us* and delivered *us* into the hands of the Midianites" (6:13).

But the Lord wanted Gideon to recognize that the presence of God with one individual was sufficient to bring deliverance to a multitude, so He answered, "Go in this *thy* might ['his might' was that the Lord was with him], and thou shalt save Israel from the hand of the Midianites" (6:14).

This statement astonished Gideon. Since he had not yet understood the import of the words that the Lord was with him, he began to look at himself. "Wherewith shall *I* deliver Israel?" (6:15) he asked, pointing to his poverty and obscurity. God explained how: "Surely I will be with thee" (6:16).

That God would deliver Israel through him seemed too good to be true, so Gideon asked for a sign. When his present of meat and cakes was consumed by the fire that sprang from the stone at the angel's touch, for the first time Gideon perceived that he had been talking with the angel of the Lord. He was filled with fear until God reassured him. And then he built an altar to the Lord.

Such was Gideon's call to be the deliverer of Israel. Next came the preparation, which consisted of tests of his faith and obedience. God's test of obedience was for Gideon to tear down the family altar erected to Baal and set up one to the Lord in its place. Then he was to offer his father's bullock upon it. Gideon did this by night. In the morning when the men of the place were ready to kill him, his father interfered. Evidently Gideon's father had been convinced of the folly of worshiping an idol that could not even defend himself. He wisely challenged, "Will ye plead for Baal? Will ye save him? ... If he be a god, let him plead for himself" (6:31).

Having publicly taken his stand for God and purified his house of idols, Gideon was ready for service. The opportunity soon came. Once more the Midianites swept across the Jordan in great numbers, devastating the country and spreading their tents in the valley of Jezreel. The Spirit of the Lord came upon Gideon, and messengers hurried throughout the tribes of Manasseh, Asher, Zebulun, and Naphtali to summon the warriors to assemble for battle. But Gideon had some doubts as to whether God actually meant to deliver Israel by him. In order to be perfectly sure of his call, he asked and received repeated proofs that he was the instrument that God wanted to use.

Thirty-two thousand men responded to Gideon's summons, declaring themselves ready to fight against Midian. Then Gideon heard God say something that seemed strange: "The people that are with thee are too many for me to give the Midianites into their hands" (7:2). God knew the heart of His people and how quick they would be to take the credit for victory to themselves. The lesson He wanted to teach them was that their deliverances always came from Him and were not the result of their own might.

So Gideon was directed to announce that all who were fearful could return to their homes. Imagine how humiliating it was for Gideon to see 22,000 men, more than two-thirds of the army, confessing that they were afraid and deserting the ranks before the first battle began. They were a "brave" lot!

However, God cannot use people who constantly look at the enemy instead of at Him and are consequently filled with fear instead of faith. So it was well that they went home. Must Gideon then go against the Midianites with only 10,000 men? This was a severe test of his faith. Surely he must now look to God to do the fighting, for what could 10,000 men do against the innumerable hosts of the enemy?

But a greater shock still was coming. "The Lord said. . . . The people are yet too many" (7:4). The number was reduced to 300 by eliminating all those who knelt on the ground as they drank from a spring. The 300 who were chosen drank by using their cupped hands to carry the water to their mouths, keeping heads erect, as though to keep a constant lookout for the enemy. Israel could learn a lesson about watchfulness from this symbolic action, but the more important lesson God was teaching was that He would give deliverance to Israel in an *impossible* situation. Now it could not possibly be a matter of military strength. Three hundred men could do nothing alone, but God said: "By the three hundred men that lapped will I save you" (7:7).

The little band waited on the hill, while camped leisurely and comfortably in the valley below them the Midianites, the Amalekites, and all the children of the east were spread "like grasshoppers for multitude." It was night, but here and there a campfire was to be seen with a few soldiers on duty, ready for any possible unpleasantness that might arise from the Israelites. Perhaps they were telling stories to keep themselves awake when Gideon and his servant, hidden in the shadows, stole within hearing distance. One man was telling a curious dream that he had had about a cake of barley bread tumbling into the camp and upsetting a tent. A comrade answered, and we can imagine the tone of conviction with which the words were uttered: "This is nothing else save the sword of Gideon the son of Joash, a man of Israel: for into his hand hath God delivered Midian, and all the host" (7:14).

These words may have been greeted with a laugh by the Midianite soldiers, but Gideon had heard enough. *He* knew, if these Midianite soldiers did not, that God had sent the dream and the interpretation. Strong in faith, he returned to the 300, triumphantly announcing, "Arise; for the Lord hath delivered into your hand the host of Midian" (7:15).

The weapons of warfare used on this occasion were peculiar. Each man was supplied with a trumpet, an empty pitcher, and a lamp inside the pitcher. Their instructions were to look at their leader and do exactly as he did. Divided into three companies, they noiselessly surrounded the sleeping camp. All was ready, awaiting the signal. The second watch had just begun when the Midianites were aroused from sleep by an awful sound. Trumpets on every hand blew louder and louder, and still louder. There was a crashing sound accompanied by a glare of lights as the pitchers were broken, exposing the lamps. And here, there, and everywhere, the battle cry rang out, "The sword of the Lord, and of Gideon" (7:20).

The trumpets, the shouts, and the lights probably appeared many times magnified. The Midianites were surrounded by their enemies, with no idea of the numbers. Panic ensued. "All the host ran, and cried, and fled" (7:21). The Midianites could not distinguish the Israelites from their own men. "And the Lord set every man's sword against his fellow, even throughout all the host" (7:22).

The tide of battle rolled toward the Jordan. Gideon sent messengers ahead throughout all Mount Ephraim to take the fords; and when the enemy was in full retreat, the Israelite warriors from Naphtali, Asher, and Manasseh joined in pursuit.

Gideon with his faithful 300 went across the Jordan, following hard on the fleetest of the foe. They were using all their strength in carrying out the Lord's command to deliver Israel.

When they became faint with the long march, they asked food of the men of Succoth and then of the men of Penuel, explaining their work and the need to be sustained. But the men of these cities had so little faith in the success of the enterprise that they actually refused to give food to their own countrymen to assist them in overcoming the enemy. They fairly deserved the punishment they later received when Gideon returned successful from the war. Such people are like Christians today who have not faith enough in the success of foreign missions, even when the work and need are explained to them, to help support those who are spending their strength in obeying our Lord's last command.

This victory over the Midianites was a mighty one. "There fell an hundred and twenty thousand men that drew sword. Thus was Midian subdued before the children of Israel, so that they lifted up their heads no more. And the country was in quietness forty years in the days of Gideon" (8:10, 28).

After the victory over the Midianites, the people of Israel became carried away with enthusiasm and wanted to make Gideon their king. The human heart is prone to hero worship. God had delivered them, but they wanted to give Gideon the glory. But Gideon was noble enough to refuse the honor. He had enough spiritual discernment to perceive that a judge was only an instrument in the hand of the true King. "And Gideon said unto them, I will not rule over you, neither shall my son rule over you: The Lord shall rule over you" (8:23).

But in all this, Gideon made a serious mistake that eventually brought tragic consequences to himself, his house, and Israel. "Gideon made an ephod . . . and put it in his city, even in Ophrah: and all Israel went thither a whoring after it: which thing became a snare unto Gideon, and to his house" (8:27). Shiloh, the site of God's Tabernacle, should have been the gathering place of the people. But Shiloh was forgotten in this time of apostasy; and the people gathered to Ophrah around Gideon, rather than to Shiloh around God. Patriotism was strong, but the people were spiritually weak. Notice the fickleness of Israel: "And it came to pass, as soon as Gideon was dead, that the children of Israel turned again, and went a whoring after Baalim, and made Baal-berith their god. And the children of Israel remembered not the Lord their God, who had delivered them out of the hands of all their enemies on every side: Neither showed they kindness to the house of Jerubbaal, namely, Gideon, according to all the goodness which he had shewed unto Israel" (8:33-35). Unfaithful to God, and unfaithful to Gideon!

III. SUMMARY

As a summary exercise, write out a list of the highlights of Gideon's life.

Lesson 5

Judges 9:1–12:15

A Study in Contrasts: Abimelech and Jephthah

As soon as Gideon was dead, the Israelites turned their backs on God again and served the gods of the pagans. Thus began another dark period in Israel's history. It continued about one hundred years and was marred by apostasies and oppressions. Only by God's grace were the people spared through the ministry of various judges.

Two men are prominent in these four chapters of Judges: evil Abimelech, who pressured some Israelites to make him their king; and righteous Jephthah, one of the six judges of this period, deliverer of Gilead from the Ammonite oppression. So this lesson is a study of contrasts, as observed in Abimelech and Jephthah. The other judges of the period are only briefly mentioned.

I. ANALYSIS

First review the survey chart of Judges (page 15) and the chart *Dates of the Judges* (page 10). Items pertaining to this lesson are shown in the accompanying diagram.

Notice that seventy years, under the five minor judges Tola, Jair, Ibzan, Elon, and Abdon, are briefly referred to in Judges, whereas the narrative dwells proportionately long on the events of Abimelech's and Jephthah's offices. This is what is known as *quantitative selectivity*, whereby the biblical author purposely devotes comparatively little space to a long period of time and, conversely, much space to a brief period. The gospels illustrate this method of writing.

Keep the outline on the next page before you as you read the chapters of this lesson.

46

THE 100 YEARS FOLLOWING GIDEON'S DEATH

Book of JUDGES	ONE CHAPTER 9:1-57	FEW VERSES 10:1-5	FEW VERSES 10:6-18	1½ CHAPTERS 11:1—12:7	FEW VERSES 12:8-15

Gideon's Death

	ABIMELECH — USURPER KING — 2 Years	TOLA 23 Years	JAIR 21 Years	PHILISTINE and AMMONITE OPPRESSION — 18 Years 10:7-8	JEPHTHAH 6 Years	IBZAN 6 Years	ELON 10 Years	ABDON 7 Years

1151 — 1149 — 1126 — 1105 — 1087 — 1081 — 1075 — 1065 — 1058

B.C.

The book of Judges devotes the most space to these two stories

47

A. Rise and Fall of a False King (9:1-57)

After you have read this chapter once, try to make an outline of its main contents. Compare your outline with the following:

Abimelech made king	(9:1-6)
Abimelech challenged	(9:7-29)
Abimelech's victories	(9:30-49)
Abimelech's defeat and death	(9:50-57)

1. *Abimelech made king* (9:1-6). The name *Abimelech* (literally "the father of a king" or "my father was king") was Gideon's choice of a name (8:31). What may have been the background of this?

_____

Abimelech's mother, a concubine or handmaiden, was from Shechem. Recall the importance of Shechem in Israel's past, as to religion. Notice where this coronation was held (9:6). What evil traits in Abimelech's heart are stated or alluded to in this paragraph?

_____

_____

2. *Abimelech challenged* (9:7-29). Study closely Jotham's words in 9:7. Analyze Jotham's pungent parable and his application. Notice the first reference to God's moving against Abimelech.

3. *Abimelech's victories* (9:30-49). What victories are recorded here?

_____

_____

_____

Why would God allow these?

_____

_____

4. *Abimelech's defeat and death* (9:50-57). As you study this paragraph, keep in mind the following core that runs through it:

"But there was . . ."	(9:51)
"And a certain woman . . ."	(9:53)
"Thus God rendered . . ."	(9:56)

Develop this study further.

B. Philistine and Ammonite Oppression (10:1-18)

After the brief citation of the judgeships of Tola and Jair (10:1-5), the author of Judges describes the oppressions and miseries Israel suffered for eighteen years at the hands of the Philistines and Ammonites. Analyze carefully verses 10-16. What do these verses teach about God?

_____

_____

_____

What other spiritual truths are taught here?

_____

_____

_____

C. Jephthah (11:1–12:15)

The story of Jephthah furnishes many practical lessons on the believer's attitude in, and relationship to, different kinds of situations. Study these two chapters with this in mind, writing down the lessons that may be learned in connection with each of the following categories:

1. Unfortunate home situation (11:1-3)
2. Forgiving those who reject you (11:4-11)
3. Maintaining a testimony in the world (11:3, 9-11)
4. Wisdom and justice in dealing with God's enemies (11:12-28)
5. Keeping vows made to God (11:29-40)
6. God in the home (11:34-40)
7. Disposing of threats to the unity of God's people (12:1-6)

II. COMMENTS

A. Abimelech

Although Gideon, the fifth judge of Israel, refused to be made king by his enthusiastic countrymen, one of his sons, Abimelech, was ambitious to get that honor for himself.

Abimelech's mother was one of Gideon's maidservants from Shechem. After Gideon's death, Abimelech and his mother persuaded the men of Shechem to make him king. With a company of worthless and reckless fellows who were hired to follow him, he went to Ophrah, his father's home, and killed all his seventy brothers except Jotham, who escaped.

When Jotham heard of Abimelech's coronation he hurried to the top of Mount Gerizim, at a time when the people were gathered in the valley below. From that vantage point his voice could be heard across the valley, and the people listened intently to the strange parable he related.

Using the figure of a republic of trees electing a king, he pictured Israel's conduct. He spoke of Gideon and his sons as an olive tree, a fig tree, and a vine, who wisely refused to leave their God-appointed places of usefulness in order to reign over the trees. But he likened Abimelech to a bramble, who not only eagerly accepted the invitation but warned that he would destroy the cedars of Lebanon if the trees did not elect him king.

Finishing his parable, Jotham reminded the people that his father had risked his life to deliver the nation, but they had returned evil for good by killing his sons and making the son of his maidservant king. He told them that if what they had done was right, then they should "rejoice . . . in Abimelech," or, as someone has put it, "Much happiness may you have in this bramble-king of yours." But if it was not right, he said, "Let fire come out from Abimelech [the bramble], and devour the men of Shechem, and the house of Millo; and let fire come out from the men of Shechem, and from the house of Millo, and devour Abimelech" (9:20).

Jotham was not a prophet, but his words proved prophetic. Only three years had passed when God's judgment came upon the men of Shechem and Abimelech.

Shechem rebelled against Abimelech, and Abimelech, notified of the uprising, came against the city and destroyed it. Even those who fled into the house of their idol were burned to death. Thus the men of Shechem were eventually punished for their ingratitude and treachery toward Gideon, whom God had appointed judge of Israel.

Abimelech's judgment was just as definite and as horrible. Fighting against the city of Thebez, he was mortally wounded by a woman who threw a piece of millstone from above, hitting him on the head. To avoid the shame of being killed by a woman, he had his armor-bearer slay him. "Thus God rendered [requited] the wickedness of Abimelech, which he did unto his father, in slaying his seventy brethren" (9:56).

B. Tola

Tola was the sixth judge of Israel. Although he judged Israel twenty-three years, only two verses, (10:1-2) are devoted to his rule. We are only told these seven facts, briefly stated, of this judge: his father's name and that of his grandfather, the tribe to which he belonged, where he lived, the length of his judgeship, his death, and where he was buried. Shamir was probably located near Jezreel.

There seems to have been peace in the land during his time, as no mention is made of wars.

C. Jair

Jair was the seventh judge. There is also little written about him. He was a Gileadite, judged Israel twenty-two years, and had thirty sons who rode on thirty ass colts and owned or ruled thirty Bedouin settlements. The possessions of Jair and his sons must have been extensive.

During the rules of Tola and Jair—forty-five years in all—Israel seems to have been free from war. But instead of being grateful to God for this blessing and obeying His Word, the people "did evil again in the sight of the Lord" (10:6). Notice the seven kinds of gods that they served (10:6).

When the Lord in His righteous indignation again chastised them, this time by allowing the Philistines and Ammonites to crush and oppress them sorely, they came to their senses in some measure and confessed, "We have sinned against thee, both because we have forsaken our God, and also served Baalim" (10:10). They confessed their sin with their lips, but something was still lacking. What would they do with their gods?

God called attention to the seven great deliverances that He had wrought for them (10:11-12); then He challenged them to go and cry unto those gods that they had chosen and ask them for deliverance. But when it came to a question of power, Israel knew how useless it was to appeal to wood and stone. None but the living God could give them aid in the time of trouble. They evidently became aware that confession involved more than admission of sins committed, for we read, "And they put away the strange gods from among them, and served the Lord" (10:16).

D. Jephthah

Jephthah was Israel's eighth judge. Few nobler characters than Jephthah are sketched in the Bible. He is mentioned among the worthies of the nation in Hebrews 11, and we see from this narrative in Judges that he was a tender, loving father, a forgiving brother, a man true to his promise, a brave and wise warrior, and a man greatly used of God.

The illegitimate son of Gilead, Jephthah was driven from home by his brothers. He went to live in the land of Tob (probably northeast of Gilead). When the Ammonites, who had long oppressed Israel, gathered their armies for war, Israel was determined to resist. But they had no one to take command.

Knowing how mighty a warrior Jephthah was, his brothers went to Tob and offered him permanent leadership if he would go with them to battle against the Ammonites. Jephthah accepted their proposition. He first tried to settle the trouble with the Ammonites by arbitration, sending messengers to the Ammonite king to inquire why he had come to fight. The king replied that when Israel had come out of Egypt they had taken land on the east of Jordan, which belonged to his nation. He demanded that the land be restored peaceably. Jephthah told him that was not true. The land Israel had taken had not belonged to either Ammon or Moab; when Israel had come out of Egypt, they had encompassed the land of Edom but had not gone within its border. The land they had taken as God had delivered it into their hands was that land that had been occupied by the Amorites, not the Ammonites. Jephthah argued with them thus:

"Wilt not thou possess that which Chemosh thy god giveth thee to possess? So whomsoever the Lord our God shall drive out from before us, them will we possess.... Wherefore I have not sinned against thee, but thou doest me wrong to war against me: The Lord the Judge be judge this day between the children of Israel and the children of Ammon" (11:24, 27).

But the king would not listen to reason, and war was declared. Jephthah fought with Ammon, and God gave Israel a great victory.

Jephthah had vowed to God that if He would give him victory he would offer as a burnt offering the first thing that came forth from his door to meet him on his return from battle. After the battle was over and the victory won, Jephthah returned with his warriors. The sight he saw at his house made Jephthah's heart stand still and the color fade from his face. Coming from the house to meet him with timbrels and dances, was his daughter, his beloved and only child. He remembered his vow.

Jephthah's daughter seems to have had the same nobility of character and loyalty to God that characterized her father, for she raised no objection when she heard of the vow. She only asked that the execution of the vow be postponed two months, during which time she could bewail her virginity. "And it came to pass at the end of two months, that she returned unto her father, who did with her according to his vow that he had vowed: and she knew no man" (11:39).

The controversial question has always been: Did Jephthah slay his daughter? At face value the record seems to justify the belief that he actually killed her. Verses 31b and 39a point to this. Those who hold this view explain the bewailing over virginity as grief over dying childless—a great disgrace to a Hebrew woman.

The other view is that Jephthah did not slay his daughter but consigned her to perpetual maidenhood, probably to serving in the Tabernacle. There are some good reasons for favoring this latter view. In the first place, Jephthah, being a godly man, must have known that the Mosaic law gave no place for human sacrifice. Some say he had "a pious but unenlightened conscience"; but an Israelite even indifferently instructed in the books of Moses could hardly be "unenlightened" to the extent of offering human sacrifice.

Second, Jephthah's daughter does not bewail her death but her virginity (11:37). Her grief is not that she must die but that she must live the rest of her life unwedded, which would be the case for any woman devoted to the service of the Lord at the Tabernacle. Third, the narrative does not say that Jephthah actually killed her. And if he did, by what altar or by what priest would such a sacrifice have been made to Jehovah? Evil as they had become, Israel had not descended to human sacrifices offered to God. Gleason Archer, Jr., writes, "The pathos of the situation in this instance did not lie in Jephthah's daughter devoting herself to divine service, but rather in the sure extinction of Jephthah's line, since she was his only child. Hence both he and she bewailed her virginity. There was no human sacrifice here."[1]

With the opening of the twelfth chapter we see the tribe of Ephraim again finding fault. They apparently were a hard lot to please. When Joshua divided the land, they were not satisfied with what they received (Josh. 17:14-18); then when Gideon went out to fight against the Midianites the feelings of the Ephraimites were hurt because they had not been invited earlier to join in the conflict (8:1); and now they come and find fault with Jephthah (12:1). Jephthah did not pacify them as did Gideon. After charging them with failure to respond to his call for help, a fight ensued in which Jephthah seized the fords of Jordan, apprehended any escaping Ephraimites, and at the end of it all the number of Ephraimites slain was 42,000.

After six years of serving Israel as their judge, Jephthah died.

1. *A Survey of Old Testament Introduction* (Chicago: Moody Press, 1964), p. 267.

E. Ibzan

Ibzan, the ninth judge of Israel, was from Bethlehem. This may have been either the Bethlehem of Judah or the Bethlehem of Zebulun near Nazareth. "Ibzan seems to have made it a practice to strengthen his political ties by marrying his children into families at a distance from Bethlehem."[2] Ibzan judged Israel seven years.

F. Elon

Elon, Israel's tenth judge, was another of the minor judges, who were also known as civil judges because they did not serve in war. Elon was from Zebulun in the north and judged Israel ten years.

G. Abdon

Abdon, Israel's eleventh judge, served eight years. Josephus writes that because Abdon's reign was a peaceful one, therefore "he had no occasion to perform glorious actions." What are your reactions to this observation? Do you recall the beatitude about peacemakers? (Matt. 5:9).

III. SUMMARY

The Scripture passage for this lesson deals mainly with the two contrasting characters Abimelech and Jephthah. As a summary exercise, compare the lives of these two men.

ABIMELECH	JEPHTHAH

2. Charles F. Pfeiffer and Everett F. Harrison, eds., *The Wycliffe Bible Commentary* (Chicago: Moody, 1962), p. 256.

Lesson 6

Birth of Samson

We have arrived at the last of Israel's seven great oppressions during the period of the judges. This seventh oppression—the Philistine—was of forty years duration; its cause was the same as always before: "The children of Israel did evil again in the sight of the Lord" (13:1). The judge raised up to deliver Israel this time was Samson, the last of the major judges. In this lesson we will be studying about his parents, his birth, and God's sovereign purpose for his life.

Before reading further, refer to the two charts *Dates of the Judges* (page 10) and *Survey of Judges* (page 15) to see how the four chapters (13-16) about Samson fit into the overall story of the judges. Also refer to the map (page 7) to see how close Dan (the "southern" Dan) was to Philistia. Zorah was located about seventeen miles west of Jerusalem.

I. ANALYSIS

As you read this chapter, observe paragraph divisions at verses 1, 2, 8, 15, 24. Mark these in your Bible. On paper draw a rectangle for recording your analytical studies, as shown by the accompanying chart. As you analyze this chapter, record your observations on the chart. (You will find it helpful to record only the biblical phrases within the rectangle, using the margins for all notations, outlines, etc.)

1. Record your own paragraph titles in the upper right-hand corner of each paragraph.

2. How do the first and last paragraphs serve as introduction and conclusion, respectively?

THE BIRTH of SAMSON
JUDGES 13

1 PHILISTINES	INTRODUCTION
2 NAZIRITE THE CHILD —Nazirite unto God	Emphases The child
8 HOW? teach us WHAT we shall do HOW	What—how?
15 FLAME unto the Lord	the Lord
24 THE WOMAN SAMSON THE CHILD THE LORD THE SPIRIT **25**	CONCLUSION

3. Study the three middle paragraphs closely. What is the main subject of each? In other words, what is being spotlighted in each paragraph? (This might be a person, thing, action, idea, etc.) Spend a lot of time on this project, for you will discover many wonderful truths in the process of study. Compare your study with the list of prominent words printed in the accompanying chart.

4. See 13:2-7. Review the Nazirite vow of Numbers 6:1-21. Observe the two principles of separation involved: separation *from* and separation *unto*. What is prominent in this paragraph of Judges?

_____

_____

How long was Manoah's son to remain a Nazirite?

_____

What is implied by the words "he shall *begin* to deliver Israel"?

_____

_____

5. See 13:8-14. What does this paragraph reveal about Manoah's heart attitude?

_____

_____

6. See 13:15-23. What good qualities of Manoah and his wife are shown here?

_____

_____

_____

In what different ways is the Lord shown to be the prominent Person?

_____

_____

_____

7. See 13:24-25. What does the phrase "at times" teach concerning the special ministry of the Spirit with the judges?

_____

_____

As of this chapter, are there any indications that Samson would become a vascillating and compromising man? What things were in Samson's favor as he arrived in this world?

_____

_____

_____

8. List the important spiritual lessons taught by this chapter.

_____

_____

_____

_____

_____

II. COMMENTS

The oppressions that God sent to punish Israel came in different regions of their Canaan homeland. The judges that God raised up to deliver Israel from the oppressions were active. Many of Israel's oppressions were in the north and also east of the Jordan. The most severe and lasting one was in the south, having the Philistines as the enemy. The Philistine oppression cited in 13:1 lasted one generation, but actually there was a continual threat from this enemy until the time of King David.

"The Philistines were intensely religious, celebrating their victories in the house of their idols [1 Sam. 31:9], often carrying their gods into battle [2 Sam. 5:21]. Dagon, 'the fish god,' was represented with the face and hands of a man and the tail of a fish [1 Sam. 5:4]. They also worshiped Ashtaroth [1 Sam. 31:10], corresponding to the ancient Assyrian goddess of propagation, Ishtar, as well as Baal-zebub ['lord of the divine abode,' 2 Kings 1:2]. Beelzebub in Jewish theology became 'the prince of the demons' [Matt. 12:24]. Philistinism, therefore, represents religionism intermixed with paganism, mere empty ritualism without regenerating and sanctifying power, since the Philistines were uncircumcised, and hence with no covenant knowledge of God or of atoning sacrifice or forgiveness of sins."[1]

In Zorah, a secluded mountain village west of Jerusalem, lived Samson's mother and father, humble earnest people who

1. Merrill F. Unger, *Unger's Bible Handbook* (Chicago: Moody, 1966), p. 176.

worshiped God. Amid all the sin, apostasy, and idolatry into which the nation of Israel had fallen were some families who still remained true to the God of Abraham. It is refreshing to catch glimpses of their faith and obedience here and there. This godly couple had one great sorrow; they were childless. One day the angel of the Lord appeared to the woman and announced that she would bear a son. Notice that God's plan for the character and work of this child was foretold before his birth (13:5). Samson was to be a Nazirite and a deliverer. Samson's father, Manoah, was a praying man (13:8); his prayer is one that parents would do well to echo.

When the promised son was born, his parents named him Samson ("little sun"). The name is interesting in view of the fact that Beth-shemesh, a town across the valley from Zorah, was the shrine town of the sun god. Of course Manoah was not naming his son for this god, but apparently the name *Samson* was common in this vicinity because of the shrine town.

In our next lesson we will study the spectacular feats of strength that this son of devout parents accomplished. The sad part of the story is that Samson's service to Israel was restricted by his indulgences in sin, a tragic departure from the ways of the godly home from which he had come and from the Nazirite life to which he had been dedicated.

III. SUMMARY

"And the WOMAN bare a son, and called his name Samson:
and the CHILD grew,
and the LORD blessed him" (13:24).

Exploits of Samson

Samson's career was marked by feats of miraculous power and marred by ignoble failures due to passion. In Hebrews 11:32 he is cited for his faith; toward the end of his life he surrendered his badge of the Nazirite vow to an evil woman, and his strength went from him.

Samson was different from the other judges. He led no army but performed great deeds single-handedly. More moments and acts of moral and spiritual weakness are ascribed to him than to any other judge. Samson's vacillating career was an illustration of the up-and-down cycle of Israel's spiritual life during the period of the judges.

The story of Samson is the story of two elements at work in him—the divine and the human—Jehovah and Samson. When the Spirit of God moved him, there was no achievement that he could not accomplish. But when left to himself, he was weak as a child and his enemies overcame him. The same applies to Israel and ourselves. Watch these two elements in Samson as you study these chapters.

I. ANALYSIS

There is much action and conversation in the story of Samson. Many spiritual applications can be made from these chapters. After you have read them, study the section paragraph by paragraph, identifying the main contents. Use the accompanying chart (or make a similar chart on a large piece of paper) to record these prominent items. Leave the last column (Steps of Samson's Downfall) for one of your major projects at the end of your study.
1. Observe Samson's vacillations from purity to passion. Notice the contrasts of physical strength and moral weakness. Look for

THE EXPLOITS OF SAMSON
JUDGES14-16

PARAGRAPH	MAIN CONTENTS	OPPOSITION to SAMSON	FEATS of SAMSON	WEAKNESSES of SAMSON	SPIRIT of the LORD	STEPS of SAMSON'S DOWNFALL
14:1-4						
14:5						
14:10						
14:15						
14:19						
15:1						
15:9						
15:14						
16:1						
16:4						
16:15						
16:18						
16:23						
16:28						

other contrasts in this story. In what ways did women contribute to Samson's downfall?

_____

2. *Chapters 14 and 15.* One thing leads to another here. How did it all begin?

_____

How do you reconcile 14:4 with God's command to the Israelites not to marry heathen? The "he" of 14:4 may be translated "He " (cf. Berkeley). Does this verse imply that God sponsored and blessed the proposed mixed marriage, or that He sponsored and blessed Israel's resistance against the Philistines? Do you recall other occasions when God permitted sinful actions of men to bring about His holy purpose? Notice how Samson fell for the deceit of the woman of Timnath (14:17). Compare Ephesians 6:11. It appears from 15:9-13 that Samson had not yet become Israel's judge. Where in the story was he first established as their judge?

_____

_____

3. Chapter 16. Make a list of the results in Samson's life due to his violation of the Nazirite vow.

_____

_____

What was Samson's last recorded prayer?

_____

_____

What do you think was really his heart's intent here? Was it suicide? Was he taking a stand on the side of the pagan Philistines? Was he declaring his willingness to suffer the consequences of his own sins while the Philistines received their own retribution? Or did he have something else in mind? Keep in mind verse 28 as you answer.

4. List the important spiritual applications to be made from the truths of these chapters.

_____

_____

_____

_____

II. COMMENTS

There are four striking scenes that come before us in Samson's history—two before he became judge and two at the end of his life:

1. Relations with the Philistine maiden, 14:1-20
2. Conflict and victory, 15:1-20
3. His capture, 16:1-22
4. His last feat and his death, 16:23-31

Let us consider carefully each event in Samson's life, observing how his failures and defeats came of his own sin, selfishness, and folly.

A. Relations with the Philistine Maiden (14:1-20)

Samson was an Israelite, and, moreover, he was a Nazirite. Nevertheless, when he saw a beautiful pagan girl, regardless of God's repeated commands against intermarrying with pagans and in opposition to his pious father's counsel, he determined to have her for his wife. His reason was simply "She pleases me well." Self was ruling. But in God's grace and despite Samson's sin, another power was working in Samson's life. It was God's overruling power. God would take this occasion, brought on by Samson's sin, and use it to further His glory.

On his way to Timnath Samson met a lion, the first enemy he encountered. In himself he would be no match for it, but "the Spirit of the Lord came mightily upon him, and he rent . . . [the lion] as he would have rent a kid" (14:6).

Afterward Samson told a riddle to the thirty Philistine youths at the wedding feast. In those days riddles were part of the entertainment for such occasions. If they guessed the riddle, Samson was to give each young man two garments (one for everyday use and a finer one for festive occasions); but if they failed to guess it within seven days, each was to give him two such garments.

God had commanded His people to have no dealings with the pagans around them. But here was Samson, whom God had chosen for the highest position in the nation, ready to marry a heathen girl, and feasting and jesting at Timnath with the enemies of God who already held God's people in bondage.

The riddle was too hard for the Philistines, so they threatened Samson's wife with death if she did not find out the answer for them. At first Samson kept his own counsel. But when she cried for seven days, he yielded, as any other man would have done under the circumstances, and told her the riddle. She, in turn, told her people. This time his failure was prompted by guile. But God came to Samson's aid, enabling him to kill thirty of the Philistines as a warning to that nation for treating him in such a manner.

B. Conflict and Victory (15:1-20)

Now began a series of engagements between Samson and the Philistines. Samson, angered at learning that his wife had been given to another, destroyed the Philistines' grainfields and olive groves by releasing foxes, or jackals, with burning brands tied to their tails. The infuriated Philistines retaliated by burning Samson's wife and her father. Then Samson, after killing a large number of them, escaped to Etam rock. But he was bound by his own people and delivered to his enemies. Although he could have overpowered his fellow Israelites, he wanted to avoid harming them. Therefore he requested that they would not attack him (v. 12). When he was brought to the Philistines, the Spirit of the Lord came mightily upon him. He burst the bands that held him, seized the new jawbone of an ass, and killed a thousand men with it.

It was a victorious day for Samson, but it was unlike victories of other judges. No Israelites joined the victor's song, for none had fought with him. Samson composed and sang his own song (15:16). After he acknowledged God's help and prayed for water for his extreme thirst, God answered his prayer. Israel then claimed him as their deliverer for the next twenty years.

C. Samson's Capture (16:1-22)

We come now to the closing scenes of Samson's career—his capture and eventual death, which were the result of indulged sin. First he played with sin in the city of Gaza, where he had illicit relations with a harlot. He escaped the enemy's plot by his God-given strength, but he was not right with God. In his heart he had already departed from his Nazirite vow of separation and purity, and his downfall swiftly followed.

But Samson's passion had not yet been satiated. The next woman in his life, Delilah of the valley of Sorek, brought on his end.

Because of Samson's infatuation with Delilah, he was induced to tell her the secret of his power. Three times he evaded the truth; but she persisted in questioning him, allowing him no rest until he finally was so tired of it that he told her his secret. When his locks were shorn, his strength left him. His strength was the Lord, and he did not know that the Lord had departed from him.

Of course his strength lay not in his long hair but in the fact that God was with him. But God was with him only as long as he kept his Nazirite vow, one law of which was that the hair must be allowed to grow.

Left to himself, Samson was helpless in the hands of his enemies. "The Philistines took him, and put out his eyes, and brought him down to Gaza, and bound him with fetters of brass; and he did grind in the prison house" (16:21).

Poor Samson, the God-appointed judge of Israel, was bereaved of his sight, bereaved of his liberty, bereaved of his strength, bereaved of his God—and grinding in the prison house of his enemies. And yet all this was traceable to his disobedience to God.

The story of Samson might have ended there. The "howbeit" of 16:22 suggests more to come. "Howbeit the hair of his head began to grow again after he was shaven." We would like to think that as blind Samson ground the grain in the prison house day after day, he began to come to his senses and to consider renewing his Nazirite vow. Whatever the case, the record does tell us that God fulfilled Samson's plea for one final demonstration of supernatural strength.

D. Samson's Last Feat and His Death (16:23-31)

The scene of Samson's death is an impressive one. The Philistines assembled from all the surrounding towns to rejoice over the capture of their enemy who had held them in check for twenty years. They were offering a great sacrifice to their god Dagon to whom they credited the deliverance of their enemy. Called to make sport for them, blind Samson prayed, "O Lord God, remember me, I pray thee, and strengthen me, I pray thee, only this once, O God" (16:28).

The Lord heard and answered. Samson, with his arms around the pillars supporting the roof, bowed with the prayer upon his lips. Although he himself died, God was glorified in that His power was manifested, his enemies were destroyed, and the pagans were shown that their idol, Dagon, was nothing.

During his twenty years as judge of Israel, Samson was not able to subdue the Philistines, but he did restrain their activities by confronting them with the mighty power of Israel's God. Probably of more value was the fact that he stirred the Israelites to see that they must attempt to rout the enemy, not live with him.

One thing was sure: the surviving Philistines would not soon forget what this lone warrior accomplished before their eyes. "Anguish and mourning reigned among them. Everything was in confusion—their princes were dead. And so the corpse of the hero who smote them more fearfully in death than in life, was borne in silent procession along their borders."[1]

III. SUMMARY

Many aspects of Samson's career illustrate the history of Israel. By way of summary for this lesson, notice some of the parallels:

SAMSON	ISRAEL
1. Before Samson's birth, God's plan for his life was revealed. He was to be a Nazirite, and deliverance was to come through him.	1. Before Israel's birth, God revealed His plan for the nation to Abraham. Israel was to be separated unto God, and the Deliverer of mankind should come through it.
2. While Samson kept his Nazirite vow, he had miraculous power over his enemies.	2. As long as Israel knew separation and consecration under Joshua, they had power over their enemies.
3. Again and again Samson tempted God by his disobedience and immoral ways.	3. Israel repeatedly rebelled against the goodness of God by departing from Him and serving idols.
4. Each time Samson was bound by his enemies, God's strength delivered him.	4. Each time Israel was in bondage to their enemies, God delivered them.
5. There came the day when Samson tempted God once too often, and his strength left him for a season.	5. Israel tempted God once too often in their rejection of the Messiah, therefore God has left them for a season.
6. Samson's enemies took him captive, blinded him, made him their servant, and mocked him.	6. In a sense Israel is a captive of their enemies today, for they are blinded and scattered and mocked by the Gentiles.
7. When Samson turned to the Lord and prayed for one more opportunity to serve Him, God granted his prayer and glorified Himself.	7. In the last days Israel will turn in repentance to the Lord and serve and glorify Him as their King.

1. John P. Lange, *Lange's Commentary on the Holy Scriptures*, P. Schaff, ed. (Grand Rapids: Zondervan, 1956), p. 225.

Idolatry of Dan

The concluding section of Judges concerns the sinful ways of two of the smaller tribes of Judah, Dan and Benjamin, both of which were located between the strong and influential tribes of Ephraim and Judah. This section, which we will study in two lessons, is called Double Appendix in the survey chart. Refer to the survey chart of Judges (page 15) to fix in your mind the relation of chapters 17-21 in the structure of the whole book.

The story about Dan concerns that tribe's religious corruption in the form of idolatry, whereas the story about Benjamin concerns immorality and national lawlessness that almost brought about the annihilation of the tribe.

As we pointed out in our survey of Judges, the action of these five chapters of the Double Appendix took place some time during the early years of the judges. As shown by the chart *Dates of the Judges* (page 10), we are following the view that dates these events during Othniel's judgeship. Whatever the dates were, these last chapters of Judges revert back to the years of the judges, in order to describe more of the corrupt ways of the Israelites, which was one of the reasons for the judges' ministry. In these two stories the Holy Spirit reveals the inner life of the people of that time in order that we may know the deeper and true reason for a long record of sin and failure.

I. ANALYSIS

First read through the two chapters, noting atmosphere, key words and phrases, and overall theme. Jot down some of your observations. Record your paragraph titles on the accompanying chart.

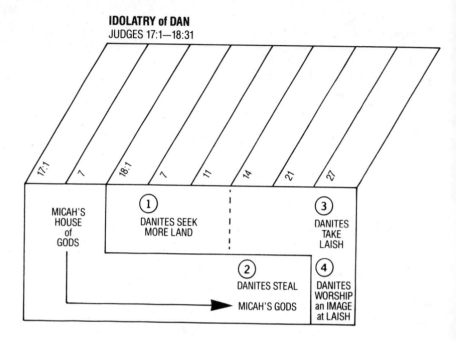

IDOLATRY of DAN
JUDGES 17:1—18:31

MICAH'S HOUSE of GODS

① DANITES SEEK MORE LAND

③ DANITES TAKE LAISH

② DANITES STEAL ➔ MICAH'S GODS

④ DANITES WORSHIP an IMAGE at LAISH

1. Observe that the tribe of Dan does not appear in the narrative until chapter 18. How then is chapter 17 related to chapter 18?

_____

_____

2. Observe from the chart how the story of Micah merges with the story of the Danites. Confirm this in your own analysis of the chapters. Observe how 18:30-31 describes the tragic climax to this story.

3. Compare the phrase "sought . . . an inheritance" (18:1) with the phrase "set up the graven image" (18:30). How are covetousness and idolatry related?

_____

_____

4. See 17:1-6. What different characteristics of *religiosity* do you see here?

_____

_____

Micah's "house of gods" was probably a shrine attached to Micah's dwelling, to which people came to ascertain the divine will. Compare 20:18 for the right source of counsel. How is verse 6 a commentary on the five verses preceding it?

_____

_____

5. See 17:7-13. Verse 13 reveals how highly the office of priest was esteemed. How is this true of religions of the world today?

_____

_____

One of Micah's sons was a priest (17:5), but the priest of verse 13 is a Levite (though probably not a Levitical priest). Observe from Micah's words that Micah was not anti-Jehovah as such; he was trying to worship and serve Jehovah through externals and images of his own making. This was idolatry.

6. See 18:1-13. The three paragraphs of these verses describe the Danites' quest for more land. Locate Laish on the map (page 7). The territory originally allotted to Dan by Joshua was small but productive. (What created a problem for Dan was the occupation of much of its land by the Philistines, which the Danites failed to conquer.) Compare this story with that of the Israelites' spying out the land of Canaan during their wilderness journey.

7. See 18:14-31. Analyze closely verses 24-26. Note the idolatry exposed by Micah's words, "Ye have taken away my gods which I made, and the priest, . . . and what have I more?" Study the context relating these two phrases to each other:

"my gods"   (18:24)
"thy life"   (18:25)

What do you suppose encouraged the Danites to set up Micah's graven image and appoint priests to serve in their worship? (18:30). Why does the narrator of Judges add the phrase "all the time that the house of God was in Shiloh" (18:31)?

_____

_____

_____

Compare 1 Samuel 1:3 and 1 Kings 12:29.

8. Write a list of some of the important spiritual lessons taught by these chapters.

_____

_____

_____

_____

_____

II. COMMENTS

The religious decay into which Israel had fallen can be seen by the narrative in chapters 17 and 18. If we compare the method of worship with the directions God gave at Sinai, it is obvious that everything was in wild confusion. God had said: "Thou shalt not make unto thee any graven image"; here idols were being manufactured in abundance. God had said that none but the sons of Aaron should be priests; here Micah's son, who was a Levite (17:5, 12), and others (18:30), were occupying the priestly office. Moreover, note that whereas God had said the Tabernacle should be the center of worship, here priests were ministering anywhere. This state of affairs was far from God's ideal. The Tabernacle was ignored and deserted, the priests set aside, Levites and common people occupying the priest's place, idols worshiped instead of God. The secret of all this confusion is found in 17:6: "In those days there was no king in Israel, but every man did that which was right in his own eyes."

There should have been a king in Israel. That is to say, God should have been King and His Word law. The human heart always needs some fixed principle as its guide. And that principle must be faith and obedience to God; otherwise man is sure to go astray. When one does that which is right in his own eyes, it is sure to be wrong in God's eyes. That is why God has revealed His will at such length in the Bible and has insisted repeatedly and emphatically that we hear, learn, keep, and obey it.

As God at Mount Sinai gave Moses the pattern for the Tabernacle, so in the Bible He gives us the pattern for our lives, our work, and our worship. Each one of us should see that we are doing all things in accordance with the pattern shown us in His Book. Failure to do this is causing confusion and error among God's children today.

"All the time that the house of God was in Shiloh" (18:31). What tender pathos in these words! It's as though God, with

70

grieved heart, were patiently waiting in His forgotten house at Shiloh for Israel to return from their idols, their man-made priests, and their own inventions, to do His holy will, adore and worship *Him.*

The heart of God must be seriously grieved today as He looks at His children living far from His ideal. They bring their own inventions into their worship and do what is right in their own eyes rather than closely following God's pattern for them.

III. SUMMARY

This is the story of a man, Micah, and a tribe, Dan. A few comparisons may serve as a summary:

MICAH	DAN
—wanted God's favor (17:13)	—wanted more land (18:9)
—set up images to help him get it	—stole images to help them get it
—the end was **frustration**: he returned to his house without his gods (18:26)	—the end was **separation**: they dwelt in a new land, worshiping new gods at Dan, but the house of God was in Shiloh (18:31)

Immorality and Lawlessness of Benjamin

This is the tragic story of the near destruction of the tribe of Benjamin. From it we learn more of Israel's utter corruption, which ultimately led to the division of the kingdom after the death of Solomon.

Two kinds of sin are especially involved in this passage: the first is of the *moral* realm; it brought on the second, of the *political* realm, which involved the law of tribal unity.

I. ANALYSIS

Follow your study procedures, which should include first reading the passage in one sitting. Record your paragraph titles on the accompanying chart. After you have done this, look for groupings of paragraphs according to subject. Make your own survey outline before studying the accompanying chart.

1. Note where the tribe of Benjamin first gets involved in the action. Compare this with the story of Dan in chapters 18-19.

---

2. How do you account for the Benjamites' refusal of 20:13*b*?

Were the other tribes justified in their demand? (20:13*a*)

---

3. Who is given credit for smiting Benjamin?

IMMORALITY and LAWLESSNESS of BENJAMIN
JUDGES 19:1—21:25

THE CRIME	RETALIATION	RESISTANCE	RETRIBUTION		RESTORATION	A COMMENT
19:1, 10, 16, 22	27, 20:1	12	17, 24	30, 36	21:1, 8, 13, 16	25
A CASE of IMMORALITY AND LAWLESSNESS		BENJAMIN RESISTS	THE BATTLE	BENJAMIN SMITTEN		CAUSE of IMMORALITY AND LAWLESSNESS
	TRIBES SEEK to PUNISH the CRIMINALS —but FAIL				TRIBES SEEK to PRESERVE BENJAMIN —and SUCCEED	

"and it came to pass" 19:1
"when there was no king" 19:1

"there was no king" 21:25
"every man did that which was right in his own eyes" 21:25

Why did God grant victories to Benjamin in the early stages of battle?

_____

_____

4. What does chapter 21 reveal of the good motives of the tribes concerning Benjamin?

_____

_____

5. What are some bright lights appearing now and then throughout these dark chapters? Spend much time on this study.

_____

_____

_____

_____

6. What are the prominent teachings of this passage for Christian living today?

_____

_____

_____

_____

II. COMMENTS

Among other things, this story reveals that Israel had fallen just as low in their moral life as they had in their devotional life during the years of the judges. This is not surprising, for spiritual health determines the morality of the ways of a man.

Here is a glimpse of the horrible depths to which human nature is capable of falling. The fact that such sins were allowed to go unpunished and were even defended by the tribe of Benjamin (20:12-14), shows that it was not the men of Gibeah alone who condoned such conduct.

This shameful wickedness seems to have aroused Israel to their senses and to have opened the eyes of the people to the depths toward which they were drifting. Did they recall the judgments of God in the Flood and in the fires of Sodom? A council of all the tribes of Israel was held, and it was decided that the offenders must be punished.

The refusal of the tribe of Benjamin to surrender the criminals to the Israelites for punishment resulted in worse consequences than would have been meted out for the crimes alone. The execution of a number of sons of Belial would have been small compared to the nearly thirty thousand Benjamites slain, not to mention the larger number of casualties. The sin of Benjamin *as a tribe* of the family of God to refuse to punish crime and to choose rather to "battle against the children of Israel" (20:14) —their brethren—was a sin of far-reaching consequences. Thus verses 20:13-14 are the critical verses of this last section of Judges.

When Benjamin declared war on Israel, the "children of Israel arose, and went up to the house of God, and asked counsel of God" (20:18). That was a move in the right direction. But perhaps to teach them how strong and deep-seated evil had become among them and to test the reality of their determination to put it away, God twice allowed Israel to be overcome by Benjamin. Each time the Israelites asked counsel of the Lord. Notice how their earnestness kept increasing. First they simply went to the house of God and asked counsel (20:23). The next time they went up and wept before the Lord till evening and then asked His counsel (20:23). The third time they not only went up and wept but they sat before the Lord and fasted until evening and offered burnt offerings and peace offerings (20:26). In this connection remember the significance of the burnt and peace offerings (see Leviticus). This time the Israelites were victorious, and the tribe of Benjamin was utterly subdued.

Men, women, and children were all slain, with the exception of 600 men who escaped to the rock Rimmon, where they abode four months. During those four months the anger of Israel was somewhat abated. They began to realize that one of the original twelve tribes of Israel would soon be extinct, for all the tribes had sworn by the Lord that they would not allow their daughters to marry the Benjamites. However, when they found that the men of Jabesh-gilead had not come up to the house of the Lord at this critical time, they resolved to punish the men by death. At the same time they decided to provide the Benjamites with wives by giving them maidens of Jabesh-gilead. Also, 200 Benjamites at a feast in Shiloh were allowed to "catch" and marry young daughters of Shiloh. Thus the difficulty about wives for the Benjamites was overcome, and the Israelites had kept their vow not to *give* their daughters to them.

Though these last chapters of Judges paint a dark picture of sin and judgment, there are these few bright spots of hope: (1) the tribes sought punishment for the criminals; (2) God gave victory to the tribes for their righteous cause; and (3) the tribes prevented the extinction of the tribe of Benjamin their brother. And who can overlook the touching episode of an old man who outshone his contemporaries in the art of hospitality by saying to a stranger, "Let all thy wants lie upon me; only lodge not in the street" (19:20)?

SUMMARY OF THE BOOK OF JUDGES

After winning the battle against Benjamin and solving the problem that ensued, the Israelites returned to their homes, "every man to his tribe and to his family" (21:24). Such a closing verse might give the impression that a new day had dawned for Israel and that in the future they would wholly obey the Lord, drive out the enemies from their land, and enjoy the blessings of their rest-land inheritance. But, as if to avoid such an impression from verse 21:24, the writer of Judges in the next verse repeated the comment he had made earlier (17:6), as his conclusion to the book: "In those days there was no king in Israel: every man did that which was right in his own eyes" (21:25). In this verse the writer was referring to all that went before, but the verse was also prophetically descriptive of the next era that Israel entered, a half millennium of kings. Before God set His nation aside, He was to prove them under human kings. But even with kings, the people would do what was right in their own eyes. In the books of Samuel we have the beginning of the record of these kings.

We have dwelt much on the darkness and corruption of the apostate years of Israel, between the conquest of Canaan under Joshua and the days of Samson. Some react to the "wild barbarity" of the stories of Judges and ask what place the book has in the story of redemption. Why does the record only briefly mention the long periods of rest? The answer is to be found in the fact that this is a book of judges (*shophetim*) who were essentially deliverers of the people from the bondage of their enemies. No doubt many beautiful stories could have been written about the rest years, but this book was especially intended to report the troublesome years. It shows God pouring out His wrath upon sinners but delivering His children from trouble and restoring them to fellowship once again when they cried unto Him.

Lesson 10
Story of Ruth

The biblical history of the period of Judges is not complete without the story of the book of Ruth. This short book is in sweet contrast to the two closing stories of the book we have just finished, but it is clear from the first verse that it belongs to this period.

The period of the judges, extending from about 1375 B.C. to 1050 B.C., was mainly one of apostasy, unrest, wars, and judgments. But there were at least temporary periods of deliverance and peace from the harassments of the enemies. The book of Ruth relates one story of the brighter years, reminding us, among other things, that there were also good people living and happy events occurring during those years.

This account of a godly family from Bethlehem reveals something of God's mysterious and wonderful ways of sovereign grace in fulfilling His divine purposes through a believing remnant. As one writer says, "The absence of any reference to 'the shield, the sword and the battle,' the atmosphere of simple piety that pervades the story, the sense throughout of an overruling providence, and the setting in that quiet corner of Judah all conspire to remind us that the story comes straight from the heart of that Hebrew consciousness of *divine destiny* that was later to reach so glorious a fulfillment."[1]

This is the only instance in the Bible in which a whole book is devoted to the domestic history of a woman. But Ruth, an ancestress of Christ, was the Mary of the Old Testament. The chief purpose of the book is to be found in the genealogical table at the end. Probably the events recorded there occurred near the close of the period of the judges. (See chart *Dates of the Judges*, page

1. G. T. Manley, ed., *The New Bible Handbook* (Chicago: InterVarsity, 1949), p. 166.

10.) God was soon to allow Israel to have kings, and so, by way of preparation, the book of Ruth introduces the kingly line. Boaz and Ruth were the ancestors of King David through whom came the Saviour-King.

Whenever God writes the history of a life, He does it with this purpose: to teach some lesson or illustrate some truth. The fact that God selected a few men and women out of the millions living at the time, and has preserved a record of their sayings and doings throughout all these centuries, ought to be sufficient evidence that there is something of vital importance hidden below the surface of the mere narrative. Therefore, in our study of the biographies of biblical characters we should dig deeply and try to find out what it is that God would teach, praying always, "Lord, what wilt Thou have me to learn?" Let this be your prayer as you study Ruth.

I. BACKGROUND

Before studying the book itself, let us look briefly at such things as the author and the date when the book was written.

A. Date and Author

The author is not known. The book may have been written some time during the reign of King David (1011-97 B.C.). It could not have been written before then, because David's name appears in 4:17, 22. It was probably written before Solomon, David's successor to the throne, otherwise the writer probably would have included Solomon's name in the genealogy. So the author was a contemporary of David.

B. Title

The book is named after its heroine, Ruth. The name Ruth may be a Moabite modification of the Hebrew *reeiut*, meaning "friendship, association."

C. Place in the Canon

Ruth follows Judges in our canon, placed there to fit the chronological sequence. In the Hebrew Bible it appears in the third division ("Writings") of the threefold canon, under a group of five books called *Megilloth* (Song of Sol., Ruth, Lam., Eccl., Esther). These books are read by the Jews at annual feasts or holidays in the Jewish calendar. The harvest-field setting of Ruth makes it an appropriate liturgy for the harvest festival (Pentecost).

D. Main Purposes of the Book

Four of these may be cited here:

1. *Genealogy*. The book introduces a few of the ancestors of David, the royal lineage of Christ the Messiah. Prominent is the inclusion of a non-Israelite (Moabitess Ruth) in this line.

2. *Typology*. The kinsman-redeemer (Boaz) is the prominent messianic type. Ruth then is a type of the church, the bride of Christ. Some scholars view Naomi as a prominent type of Israel.[2] Other types may be seen in the book.

3. *Theology*. Underlying the entire book is its revelation of the character and ways of God: His providence, sovereignty, grace, and holiness, and His invitation of salvation to all peoples.

4. *History*. As noted earlier, the book describes a few intimate experiences of a godly family of Bethlehem during the period of the judges.

II. THE STORY OF RUTH

In this lesson we will concentrate on studying what the book of Ruth says. In the concluding lesson we will dwell on what the book is intended to mean and teach.

First, read through the four chapters at one time. If possible, read aloud. Familiarity with the text is the first law of Bible study. Have pencil or pen in hand as you read so that you can make notations in your Bible along the way. After this reading, consider these:

1. What are your major impressions?

_____

_____

2. How does the story compare with those of Judges?

_____

3. Any key words and phrases?

_____

4. Could you retell the story after this reading?

2. For a thorough treatment of this interpretation, see Merrill F. Unger, *The New Unger's Bible Handbook* (Chicago: Moody Press, 1966, 1984), pp. 141-42.

5. What place does God have in the lives of the main characters?

_____

_____

_____

6. What is the tone of the book?

_____

_____

7. What is the main subject of each of the four chapters?

_____

_____

_____

_____

You will find this to be an interesting study, for it will lead to various studies of types later when you look for the truths taught by the book.

It will be beneficial for you to record some of your observations. Follow the suggestions given below.

1. Record a chapter title and paragraph titles on the next page.

2. Record these items: geography, action, and the parts played by the three main characters. As far as possible, put this in condensed outline form. (You may find that for some outlines two chapters treat the same general subject.) Compare your outlines with the following chart.

CHAPTER	1	2	3	4
NAOMI	BEREAVED of LOVED ONES	HELPING RUTH		REJOICING over OBED
RUTH	CHOOSES	SEEKS		RECEIVES
BOAZ	—	SEES	LOVES	MARRIES

RUTH STORY of REDEMPTION

Key verses:
1:16, 4:14

CHAPTER TITLE

PARAGRAPH
TITLES

1:1-5 1:6 1:14 1:29 2:1 2:8 2:17 3:1 3:6 3:14 4:1 4:7 4:13 4:18

GEOGRAPHY   (1)   (2)   (3)   (4)

ACTION

HIGHLIGHTS of THEIR EXPERIENCES

NAOMI

RUTH

BOAZ

KEY QUESTIONS

REFERENCES
to
GOD, the LORD

3. Key questions are asked throughout the book. Record these.
4. References to "God" and "the Lord" appear often. Record these and the significance of their use.

* * *

After you have completed recording items on the chart, return to the text and closely analyze some of the key passages. Here are some suggested studies:
1. Compare the Naomi of 1:19-22 with the Naomi of 4:13-17.

_____

_____

_____

2. What spiritual lessons are taught by 1:14-18?

_____

_____

_____

3. Study carefully paragraph 4:13-17.
4. Study the genealogy note of 4:18-22. Refer to Genesis 38:29; 46:12 for the identification of Pharez. Of what significance is the fact that the name "David" is the last reference of genealogy here?

_____

_____

III. COMMENTS

Let us rehearse a few of the highlights of the story as it centers on the four main characters, Naomi, Orpha, Ruth, and Boaz.

A. Naomi

Naomi was a Jewess living in Bethlehem in the days when the judges ruled. Her husband's name was Elimelech, and her two sons were Mahlon and Chilion. Those were dark days both morally and spiritually as we have seen in our study of Judges. When God sent a famine, this family chose to move to Moab to search for food.

The account does not explicitly say that they sinned by moving to pagan Moab, but we may conclude that they sinned for at least three reasons: (1) Naomi later recognized that her bereavement of husband and sons was the judgment of God; (2) the Moabites as a nation were barred from participation in the life of Israel (Deut. 23:3-6), and the Israelites were forbidden to "seek their prosperity" (Deut. 23:3-6); (3) if God wanted His people to leave the land of their inheritance, He would have told them (as He did later in the captivities).

Famine was God's chastisement for sin and His call to repentance, as He had long before told His people. It was either an unrepentant spirit or lack of faith that made Naomi and her husband and two sons leave the land of Canaan (God's appointed place for His people) and go into the land of Moab to settle among idol worshipers. There they would be far from God's people and from God's blessing and protection, because God had promised His people neither protection nor blessing outside the land of Canaan. Canaan is where He planned for them to live, and they turned their backs on Him when they turned their backs on Canaan.

After Naomi's husband died, her two sons married pagan girls. They were probably nice, good-hearted girls, but they were certainly ignorant of God and God's ways. No doubt Naomi felt the disgrace of having these pagan alliances, but what else could she expect, having brought her sons into such society?

Then both sons died. Naomi was grief-stricken, and well she might be. She and her husband had disobeyed God in leaving Canaan, and her sons had disobeyed God in marrying pagan wives. Nothing but disappointment, trouble, loss, and death had been the result. Then someone brought word from the land of Judah that God was graciously visiting His people again in giving them bread. Naomi announced her intention to return home. She had everything to gain and nothing to lose in this decision.

B. Orpah

When Naomi began her journey back to Bethlehem, Orpah and her sister-in-law Ruth accompanied her. They may have got as far as the border of Moab when Naomi paused to explain just what it would mean for them if they continued with her. It was too late now for Naomi to bear sons who could be their husbands. She could not promise them earthly comforts or blessings. She herself was a poor old woman. Moreover they would have to give up many things. Relatives, country, friends, and especially idols would have to be left behind. Of course Naomi could promise them the presence, protection, and provision of almighty God, if they would become His people, but they themselves would have to decide which they valued most.

Orpah decided she could not give up so much. Perhaps she had not before fully considered the matter or counted the cost. If she could have taken her idols along she might have gone. But under the circumstances she said, "No," kissed her mother-in law, turned back to Moab, and was soon among her people and her idols, living as before. That is the last we hear of Orpah.

C. Ruth and Boaz

Let us follow the story of Ruth and Boaz by noting the main points of each of the four chapters of Ruth. In chapter 1 Ruth makes some big decisions. When Orpah left them, Naomi said to Ruth, "Behold, thy sister in law is gone back unto her people, and unto her gods: return thou after thy sister in law." This was the supreme moment for Ruth. She had to make the most important decision that any soul can make. Ruth may have looked toward Moab and thought of all she was leaving, and then she may have looked toward Canaan and remembered all she had been told by her Jewish husband and his relatives regarding Israel's God. By pure and simple faith she took her stand and replied, "Whither thou goest, I will go; and where thou lodgest, I will lodge: thy people shall be my people, and thy God my God" (1:16).

In this first chapter Ruth's love and loyalty to her mother-in-law is generally emphasized. Beautiful as that may be, the chief point in her decision is that she took the God of the Hebrews to be her God. (See 1:16 and 2:12.) By her decision, Ruth became one of God's people. But she did not stop with that. She was not satisfied simply to belong to God's people. When she reached God's rest-land, she wanted to enjoy and take advantage of all the privileges to which this position entitled her.

In chapter 2 we see Ruth taking advantage of God's gracious law that the poor and stranger might glean after the reapers. She lost no time in going to work in the harvest field that she afterward learned belonged to the wealthy Boaz, a near kinsman of her late husband, who had died in Moab. She did not know how kind, noble, and generous the rich kinsman was until she went to work in his field.

Chapter 3 is the story of Naomi's helping Ruth find "rest." The "rest" of 3:1 obviously refers to marriage. Concerning this, one has written: "In the East the position of unmarried women is dangerous and trying—only in the house of a husband can she be sure of respect and protection."[3]

3. Robert Lee, *The Outlined Bible* (Westwood, N. J.: Revell, n.d.).

It is a night scene. Labor has ceased. The workers have gone to their homes. Now Ruth can speak with Boaz alone and show him that she wants *him* more than she wants his *gifts*.

The manner in which Ruth's betrothal to Boaz was brought about must not be judged by Western customs and conventions. The ritual of 3:3-9 was apparently a well-recognized custom of seeking a husband in that day. There is everything about the story to indicate that the heart motives and the actions of Ruth and Boaz were pure and righteous (cf. 3:11). Boaz's advice of 3:14 was either to avoid misunderstanding by others or to withhold from the public the news of his intentions until he officially became Ruth's "redeemer" (4:9-10).

In your study of chapters 2 and 3, note the many advantages that Ruth secured through Boaz in the early days of their acquaintance. Observe such things as fellowship, protection, water, food, blessing, and relaxation.

In the last chapter we see Ruth no longer as the pagan maiden, nor the poor gleaner, but raised to the position of bride to Boaz and mother to Obed, who was the ancestor of David. When we first saw her, she was a Gentile, worshiping idols in a far country. Now she is the bride of Boaz and dwells in God's chosen land and worships Him.

* * *

Two key words of the story are "kinsman" and "redeem," which have given Boaz the classic title "kinsman-redeemer."

D. Kinsman

This word (Hebrew *gô-ēl*) appears thirteen times in Ruth. *Gô-ēl* basically means "one who redeems," and in the setting of Ruth refers to the near male relative of a deceased man who had the right and duty to buy back or redeem land that had been sold to another family, thus preventing the alienation of the land and the extinction of the family. If the nearest kinsman could not fulfill such a redemption, the next of kin (Boaz) had the opportunity. The sequence of the story was something like this:

1. When Naomi returned from Moab, she sold her deceased husband's property, probably under pressure of poverty. "Either Elimelech sold the land before he went to Moab and the year of jubilee came in in the interval so that the land reverted to Naomi

(see Lev. 25:3ff) or the land was for the last ten years left in the care of a friend."[4]

2. It was necessary for a *gô-ēl* to redeem the land in order to keep it in the family name. By buying it back, however, "the *gô-ēl* would not come into possession of the land himself, but would hold it in trust for his son by Ruth, who would inherit the name and patrimony of Mahlon (her first husband)."[5] In this connection it should be noted that it was Naomi who had prior claim upon the *gô-ēl*, but she surrendered it in favor of Ruth.

3. As it turned out, the nearest kinsman wanted the land (4:4*b*) but not Ruth and so would not gain by the transaction; Boaz wanted Ruth, not the land, and had the money to transact the business. (Cf. these references to kinsman and his right to redeem: Lev. 15:15-31, 47-55; Deut. 25:5-10; Job 19:25.)

E. Redeemer

In view of the above description, it may now be seen why Boaz is called a kinsman-redeemer. The two words are essentially synonyms, but the word "redeemer" is added since our English word "kinsman" usually suggests only the idea of family relationship. Notice the eight occurrences of the word "redeem" in chapter 4. It translates the same Hebrew root as *gô-ēl*.

IV. RECAPITULATION

See how much of the story of Ruth you can relate without referring back to the text. You will find that such a procedure will even suggest new insights into this beautiful story of redemption. This exercise will also prepare you for the next lesson, where you will study more closely the interpretations and applications of this book.

4. Francis Davidson, ed., *The New Bible Commentary* (Grand Rapids: Eerdmans, 1953), p. 261.
5. Charles F. Pfeiffer and Everett Harrison, eds., *The Wycliffe Bible Commentary* (Chicago: Moody, 1962), p. 271.

Lesson 11
Teaching of Ruth

The story of Ruth is not only a literary gem of matchless beauty but a spiritual reservoir of living water in a bleak desert. Its beauty magnifies the godly traits of its main human characters; but of deeper significance to the reader are its pictures of Christ the Redeemer, as seen in its types, symbols, and shadows, not to mention the grand fact of Christ's ancestry in the Moabitess Ruth.

Your study in this lesson will center on your search for the spiritual truths that the Holy Spirit intended this book to convey. Like all books of the Bible, the truths are numerous and of various sorts. Here is a listing of a few of the possible vantage points from which one might view this four-chapter book of great diversity.

I. TRUTHS ABOUT GOD

You began this study in Lesson 9. Pursue it further, seeing what it teaches (explicitly or implicitly) about:

A. God as the Holy One

_____

_____

_____

B. God as Judge

_____

_____

_____

87

C. God as the Worshiped One

_____

_____

_____

D. God as the Gracious Lord

(For example, how do you account for God's so honoring a Moabitish woman as to bring her into the fellowship of Israel and making her an ancestress of Christ? Compare this with the love of God in John 3:16.)

_____

_____

_____

E. God as the Rewarder

_____

_____

_____

II. TRUTHS ABOUT MAN

Look for all the good and bad qualities of man that are found here. For example, consider how the formerly pagan foreigner Ruth was treated by the Bethlehemites. (This suggests just one path of inquiry.)

_____

_____

_____

III. TRUTHS ABOUT SALVATION

The study of "salvation" in Ruth may be made in two ways: historically and typically.

A. Historically

How were people saved in Old Testament days?

_____

_____

Did Moabitess Ruth become saved?

_____

If so, on what basis?

_____

_____

Look into all the wonderful aspects of this subject as it is taught by this historical account of actual events. Then make your own topical outline of the book of Ruth, using the topic Salvation or, more appropriately for Ruth, Redemption. Record this on your chart of Ruth. Here is one example (by Unger):

Deciding by Faith	Gleaning under Grace	Communing in Fellowship	Resting in Redemption

B. Typically

Since we have the New Testament with its antitypes (antitypes are the fulfillments of types), it is usually not too difficult for us to discover types that reside in the persons, things, and events of Old Testament history. (Note: In your study of types, always be careful to make the antitype, not the type, the preeminent fact; also, avoid forcing types for the mere sake of typology.)

There is a rich underlying typology in Ruth that you will want to consider in your studies. The major groups are as follows:

1. *Ruth representing the church, the body of believers.* Follow this theme through from Ruth's lost condition in chapter 1 to her salvation in the later chapters. G. Campbell Morgan suggests an outline: The Choice of Faith (1-2); The Venture of Faith (3); The Reward of Faith (4).

2. *Boaz representing Christ, the Kinsman-Redeemer.* Gleason L. Archer says that "the little book of Ruth is one of the most instructive in the Old Testament concerning the mediatorial work of

the Lord Jesus."[1] He cites some of the qualifications and functions for the *gô-ēl*:

(a) He must be a blood relative.

(b) He must have the money to purchase the forfeited inheritance.

(c) He must be willing to buy back that forfeited inheritance.

(d) He must be willing to marry the wife of a deceased kinsman.

Pursue this study further, observing how Christ as our Kinsman-Redeemer fulfills the above qualifications.

3. *Naomi representing Israel, in her past, present, and future.* Merrill F. Unger[2] sees a host of types under this category. Some of these are:

(a) Naomi (Israel) is married to Elimelech (the Lord) and enjoys prosperity in Canaan.

(b) Naomi migrates to Moab—Israel's worldwide dispersion.

(c) Death of Elimelech—Israel's separation from the Lord.

(d) Orpah chooses to remain in Moab—unbelieving Jews remaining among the nations.

(e) Ruth chooses to return to Judah—believing remnant of Jews returning to Palestine.

(f) Ruth desires Boaz—Israel seeking after the Lord at the end-time.

(g) Boaz redeems the land and marries Ruth—the redeemed remnant enters into the blessings of kingdom rest (Isa. 4:1-6; 11:1-16; Zech. 8:6-8).

As a study exercise, read through the book of Ruth again, looking for other types of Israel as they appear between the high points listed above.

4. *Orpah representing the large Gentile world, hearing the gospel that was first given to the Jew but not believing.* Since the story of Orpah in the book of Ruth is brief, not much can be developed here. However, see what types you can find in this group.

In your study of types you often will find the literal meanings of the names of the persons to suggest some clues of interpretation. Here are the prominent names of this book, with their meanings:

> Naomi—"pleasant one"
> Elimelech—"my god is king"
> Mahlon—"sick"

1. *A Survey of Old Testament Introduction* (Chicago: Moody, 1964), p. 269.
2. *The New Unger's Bible Handbook* (Chicago: Moody Press, 1966, 1984), pp. 141-42.

Chilion—"pining"
Orpah—"neck" (i.e., "stubbornness")
Ruth—"friendship"
Boaz—"in him is strength"

IV. SPIRITUAL LESSONS TAUGHT BY RUTH

Keeping in mind the full scope of this inspired book of God, write out a list of the prominent spiritual lessons that you think the Holy Spirit is teaching today through its four chapters. Keep in mind that all Scripture is God-breathed and is profitable "for teaching, for reproof, for correction, for training in righteousness, so that the man of God may be well-fitted and adequately equipped for all good work" (2 Tim. 3:16-17, Berkeley Version).

Bibliography

COMMENTARIES AND TOPICAL STUDIES

Barber, Cyril J. *Ruth: An Expositional Commentary.* Chicago: Moody, 1983.

Bruce, F. F. "Judges." In *The New Bible Commentary*, ed. F. Davidson. Grand Rapids: Eerdmans, 1953.

Cook, G. A. *The Book of Ruth.* The Cambridge Bible. Cambridge: Cambridge U., 1913.

Cox, Samuel. *The Book of Ruth.* London: Religious Tract Society, 1922.

MacDonald, A. "Ruth." In *The New Bible Commentary*, ed. F. Davidson. Grand Rapids: Eerdmans, 1953.

Pfeiffer, Charles F. "Judges," and "Ruth." In *The Wycliffe Bible Commentary*, ed. Charles F. Pfeiffer and Everett F. Davidson. Grand Rapids: Eerdmans, 1953.

Wood, Leon. *Distressing Days of the Judges.* Grand Rapids: Zondervan, 1975.

OTHER RESOURCES

Jensen, Irving L. *Jensen's Survey of the Old Testament.* Chicago: Moody, 1978.

The New International Version Study Bible. Grand Rapids: Zondervan, 1985.,

Payne, J. Barton. *An Outline of Hebrew History.* Grand Rapids: Baker, 1954.

Pfeiffer, Charles F., and Vos, Howard J. *The Wycliffe Historical Geography of Bible Lands.* Chicago: Moody, 1967.

The Ryrie Study Bible. Chicago: Moody, 1978.

Strong, James. *The Exhaustive Concordance of the Bible*. New
   York: Abingdon, 1890.
Tenney, Merrill C. *The Zondervan Pictorial Bible Dictionary*.
   Grand Rapids: Zondervan, 1963.
Unger, Merrill F., ed. *The New Unger's Bible Dictionary*. Chicago:
   Moody, 1988.